GRAPHIC DESIGN

PART ONE – LETTERING AND TYPOGRAPHY

TONY POTTER

Designed by
IAIN ASHMAN

Lettering by
PATRICK KNOWLES

Alphabets designed by
**MICHAEL HARVEY,
JONATHAN COLECLOUGH & WILF DICKIE**

Illustrated by
STEVE CROSS

Additional illustrations by

**GUY SMITH, IAN JACKSON,
CHRIS LYON, COLIN RATTRAY,
PAUL BAMBRICK, JEREMY BANKS**

Material in this book is available separately as
Lettering and Typography and **Technical Drawing**.

Contents

First published in 1987 by Usborne Publishing Ltd,
83-85 Saffron Hill, London EC1N 8RT, England.

Printed in Great Britain.

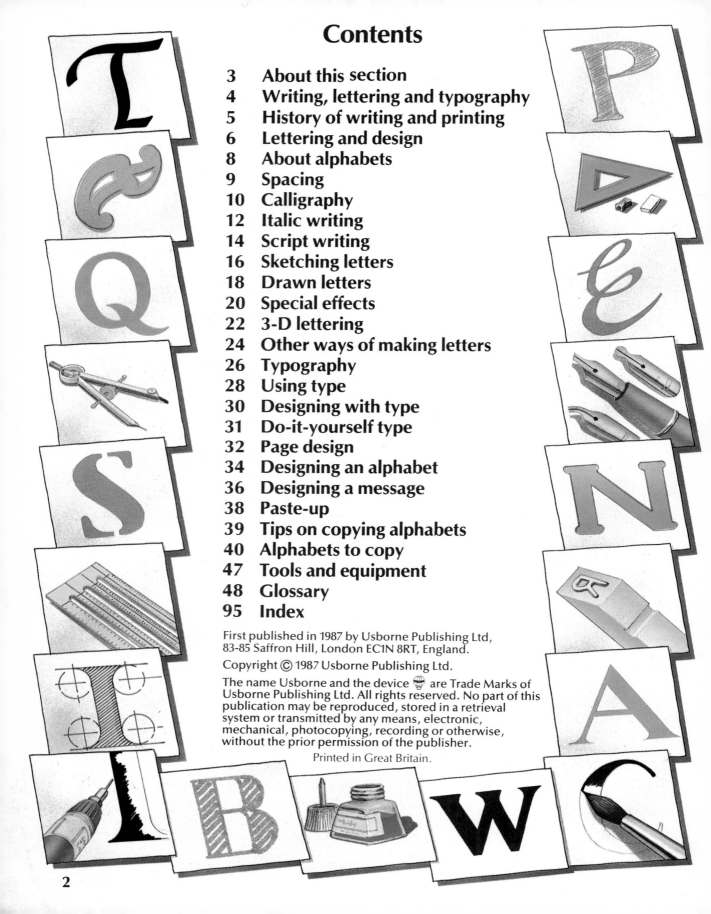

About this section

This section is a guide to the making and use of letters, or letterforms. It covers letterforms made by hand and by machine, from writing to printing. It explains the basic techniques of both handmade and machine-made letterforms, which are summarized below.

This section is divided into six parts, identified by coloured stripes at the top of the page, like this:

The yellow, pink and green parts are all about hand-lettering methods.

First you can read about the history of lettering, from ancient cave symbols to the latest computerized methods. You can also find out about special words used to describe and organize letters.

Next you can find out how to do different styles of handwriting.

- **Calligraphy, which means "beautiful writing".**
  See page 10
- **Italic handwriting – a style of calligraphy.**
  See page 12
- **Different kinds of script writing.**
  See page 14

Various ways of drawing and painting letters are explained next. There are also tips on different ways of making three-dimensional letters.

- **Sketched letters**
  See page 16
- **Drawn letters**
  See page 18
- **Distorted letters**
  See page 20
- **3-D letters**
  See page 22
- **Stencilled letters**
  See page 24
- **Cut paper letters**
  See page 24
- **Rubbings**
  See page 25
- **Sprayed letters**
  See page 25

This part of the section is all about machine-made letters. The study of this is called typography.

- **Typesetting (like the words on the pages of this book).**
  See pages 26-29
- **Typewriting**
  See page 32
- **Rub-down lettering**
  See page 32

This part of the section gives lots of tips on design and layout. Layout is how letters and pictures are organized on a page. These tips are useful whether you want to use hand or machine-made methods to do posters, greeting cards, newsletters or any other kind of message which uses words.

Finally, there are some alphabets to copy. Tips on copying alphabets are on page 39.

Glossary

This book introduces many unusual words. These are defined on page 48 and are highlighted in the book on each page where you first come across them, like this: *pica*.

Design tips

Throughout this section there are tips on design to help you make the most of your lettering. You can find them easily by looking for headings in blue like this:

DESIGN TIPS

Getting started

Few tools or materials are needed to get started with lettering – just paper and a few inexpensive pens.

The styles of lettering shown in this section are not fixed styles that you must stick to rigidly. It is a good idea just to have a go at styles you are interested in as you come across them in the book and then practise as much as possible. You will probably find you quickly develop styles of your own, based on those explained.

Guide lines

For any hand-lettering, it is a good idea to draw guide lines in pencil, as shown round the heading above, to help keep your lettering straight.

On thin paper, you can draw guide lines on the back, making it easier to erase them without smudging the lettering.

Guide lines

Writing, lettering and typography

This page shows the main ways of hand-lettering – writing and drawing – and introduces methods used in *typography*.

Letters, numbers and other characters, whether hand or machine-made, are called letterforms.

Writing

Writing is the direct creation of cursive, or flowing, letterforms made with a pen, pencil, brush or similar tool. Writing that aims to be beautiful is called *calligraphy*.

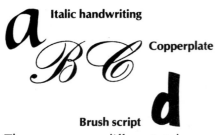

Italic handwriting

Copperplate

Brush script

There are many different styles of writing and calligraphy. Three styles, produced with different writing tools, are shown above.

Drawn lettering

Drawn letterforms are sketched or carefully constructed. There are usually three basic stages involved, shown on the right.

1 First the letters are lightly drawn in pencil. These are called *construction lines*.

2 Each letter is then revised, often by tracing the pencil lines, and then filled in with ink or paint.

3 Finally, any imperfections are corrected with white paint and a brush or a technical pen.

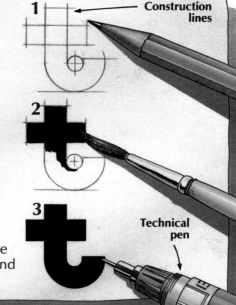

Construction lines

Technical pen

Type

Type is a letterform which has first to be drawn. It used to be cast in metal or cut in wood. Today, it is usually converted into electronic codes to produce a photographic image on paper.

The arrangement of type to form words is called typesetting.

Computer typesetting machine

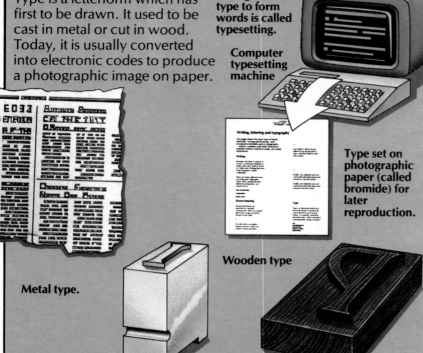

Metal type.

Wooden type

Type set on photographic paper (called bromide) for later reproduction.

Different type styles are called *typefaces*. Each complete alphabet, including numbers and punctuation marks, is called a *font* or *character set*.

1 abcdefghijklmnopqrstuvwxyz
ABCDEFGHIJKLMNOPQRST
1234567890 .,;:'' «»&!?

2 abcdefghijklmnopqrstuvwx
ABCDEFGHIJKLMNOPQ
XYZ 1234567890 12345678

3 abcdefghijklmnopqrstuvwxyz
ABCDEFGHIJKLMNOPQRST
1234567890 .,;:'' «»&!?

4 abcdefghijklmnopqrstuvw
ABCDEFGHIJKLMNOPQR
XYZ 1234567890 .,;:'' «»&!?

Above are some popular type styles. See if you can identify them by looking at the tips on page 26.*

*Answers on page 48

History of writing and printing

The history of the written and printed word is very complex. Below are some of the key developments in the western world.

20,000BC. Picture writing

Horse

Modern ideogram

Fish

Early realistic picture writing on cave walls gradually evolved into ideograms. These are symbols which represent ideas.

3000BC. Phonology

Cuneiform (from the Latin for "wedge") writing was pressed into clay with a wedge-like tool.

The first system with signs which represent sounds was used in the Middle East. This system of writing is called Cuneiform.

Ancient Greek writing

The Greeks adapted a Phoenician alphabet to create one of their own. Our alphabet is based on this.

The word "alphabet" comes from "alpha" and "beta", the first two letters of the Greek alphabet.

Ancient Roman writing

The Romans used the Greek letters A,B,E,H,I,K,M,N, O,X,T,Y,Z with few changes, added C,D,G,L,P,R,S and took three others (F,Q,V) from the Phoenicians.

Roman stone inscription.

Only capital letters existed at this time.

1st-15th centuries AD

During this time the modern alphabet, with large and small letters, gradually developed. Three extra letters (J,U,W) were added.

abcde o ßimfpst

ABEhIRLW

Pen-lettering

You can find out more about this period on page 10.

1450. Invention of type

Around 1450 Johann Gutenberg invented printing with movable type. Gutenberg's type was based on a style of handwriting popular at the time.

Page from Gutenberg's 42-line bible, about 1453-5.

1470. Roman typeface

The Venetian printer Nicholas Jenson, designed the first truly Roman *typeface*.

es nafcitur)fed n tur. Credidit eni

Jenson's typeface, which he designed in Venice.

Hand-made books

Monks in a medieval scriptorium.

Until printing was invented, books and other documents were produced in "scriptoria" — rooms full of scribes who copied pages by hand.

19th century

Hot metal typesetting machine

UNRIVALLED AT

ADMISS

ONE-SHI

Advertising typeface

Many new typefaces were designed, especially for advertising in the early 19th century. New machines to set type were invented later.

20th century. Computers and calligraphy

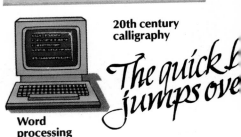

20th century calligraphy

The quick jumps ove

Word processing

Computer typesetting and word processors were invented. There was also a revival of interest in pen lettering and calligraphy.

Lettering and design

Letters are the building bricks of words and messages. What they look like, how you organize them, and their suitability for the job are the three most important things in getting a message across successfully to someone. The choice of lettering depends on the purpose of what you have to say, the people you are saying it to and where it is said.

Appearance

The appearance, or style, of lettering communicates something, just as the words themselves do, as you can see below. Style is important because it affects the interpretation and effectiveness of what you are trying to say.

Message makers

DANGER

SAFETY HELMETS MUST BE WORN BEYOND THIS POINT

Warning signs need to be clear and easy to read.

Letters have two jobs. They are both symbols which have a meaning and decorative, or abstract, shapes. In this message, the meaning of the words is more important than their abstract shapes.

Here, letters make an abstract picture, but carry no precise message. In most graphic design, the meaning of the words and their appearance are equally important.

Letters are rarely used for decoration only.

Letters are usually used to form words to say something to someone.

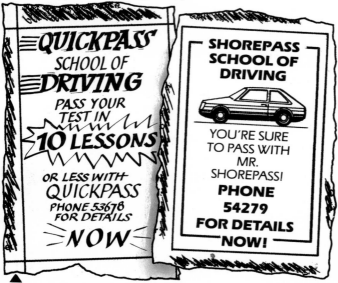

If you needed driving lessons, which of these two schools would you choose from their advertisements? Try asking ten people the same question and you will probably find they go for the one on the right. The lettering looks calmer and more technical than the one on the left, making you feel confident about the school.

Similar lettering, used in another situation, has a different effect. Which sign do you think makes the vegetables looks the fresher? The lettering on the left looks "hand-made", thus making them seem more homely and genuinely fresh than the other sign does. You could ask ten people the same question to see if they agree.

Stages in design

Organizing messages is an important part of design. The steps on the right show the basic stages involved. Before starting you need to ask what you want to say and to whom? Is your message for young or elderly people? Is it to be read close by or at a distance as people dash past? Should it look "traditional", "modern" or "flashy"?

You can find out more about planning and designing messages on pages 32-33 and 36-37.

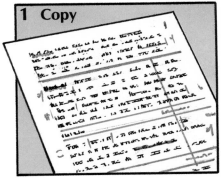

1 Copy

Words to be lettered or typeset are called *copy*. Copy often needs to be divided into chunks of words according to their relative importance.

2 Thumbnail

Thumbnails are tiny sketches, drawn in proportion to the full-size job, to work out various ways of arranging the information.

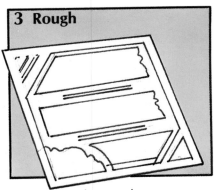

3 Rough

Designers often re-draw successful thumbnails to full size, adding colour if appropriate. This helps in refining the final idea.

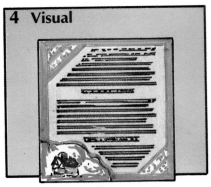

4 Visual

A visual is a well worked-out design, in colour if necessary, which gives a good idea of the finished work to show to a customer, or client.

5 Finished work

This is the finished work, ready to use, either as it is, or for subsequent printing. Finished work ready for printing is called *artwork*.

DESIGN TIPS

Organization

One of the aims of design is to achieve visual order. This means making your message clear to read and good to look at. There are several ways of achieving visual order within a block of copy, as described on the right. You can find out more about visual order on pages 30 and 37.

Copy which lines up on one side only is called unjustified.

This is ranged (or flush) left.

This is ranged (or flush) right.

Copy which lines up on both sides is called justified or flush left and right. Justified setting is nearly always used in newspapers.

This arrangement is called centred.

Words shaped around a picture have a ragged edge and are called run-arounds.

Run-arounds are often used in advertisements.

7

About alphabets

An alphabet is all the letters, numbers, punctuation marks and other characters used in a particular language. There are thousands of different styles of letterforms, used in books, papers, on signs, TV and so on.

abcde

Each letter in an alphabet is designed to look different from the others and yet form part of a whole. One letter slightly different in style from the rest stands out, as you can see above.

Letters are made to look part of a whole by designing them with certain features in common. A name is given to each of their parts, which helps designers to think and talk about them. You can find out the most important of these names on the right.

Changing any part circled in red, even by a tiny amount, would alter the letter's character.

Parts of letters

A font consists of capital letters (or upper case), small letters (or lower case), numbers, punctuation marks, and sometimes italics and small capital letters (which are the same height as the small letters).

Letters have basic parts, with special names, shown on the right.

Upright letters are also called roman.

Slanted letters are called italic.

Stem. Stroke running from top to bottom.

Curve. Any curved shape. Bowl. Continuous curve.

Serifs

Arm. Horizontal or diagonal strokes.

Bar. An arm joining two parts together.

Serifs

Serifs are strokes which finish off the ends of stems, arms and curves. A letter without serifs is called *sans serif* (or sanserif).

Serifs derive from the use of brushes and chisels and often become distinctive features of letters. Other names

Serif

Sans serif

Many serif styles have evolved since Roman times. Some of the most common are shown below.

Full bracketed | Hairline | Slab | Slab bracketed

Head | Terminal

Ascender → Ascender line →

dpaEfgP

Descender | Base line | Descender line | Foot | Tail | "x" height

History of the alphabet

The ancient Roman alphabet of 23 letters, which forms the basis of the modern alphabet, was often cut on stone. The most beautiful of these inscriptions is thought to be that at the base of Trajan's column in Rome.

SENATVSPOPVLVSQ
IMPCAESARIDIVINER
TRAIANOAVGGERMD
MAXIMOTRIBPOTXVII

Inscription at the base of Trajan's column 113-114AD. A large proportion of the Roman population could read and there were informal styles of writing on vellum and parchment.

An alternative alphabet of small letters did not begin to appear until around the end of the 8th century AD, in a style called the Carolingian minuscule.

Spacing

Without spaces, lettering or type is very difficult to read, as you can see below.

ALLTHEBOOKSINTHEENGLISH LANGUAGEHAVEBEENWRITTEN WITHJUSTTWENTYSIXLETTERS.

There are three kinds of spacing to take into account when doing any kind of lettering: letter spacing, word spacing and line spacing.

Word spacing

Word spacing is the space between words.

GOOD WORD SPACING

Leave a space the size of a small "n" between words in small letters.

mallnlett

Leave a space the size of a large "O" between words in large letters.

RGEOLET

For *justified* text, as shown on the right, leave gaps of varying sizes between the words, not the letters.

I must go down to the sea again, to the lonely sea and the sky, I left my shoes and socks there, I wonder if they're dry?

Letter spacing

This is a letter space.

Letter spacing is the space between letters. For lettering to look right, all gaps between letters must appear equal in size, although they may not actually be so.

FA

Well spaced word.

HELLO

Badly spaced word.

HELLO

You can judge by eye whether letter spacing is right by shading trial lettering as shown below.

HELLO

All shaded areas should look equal by eye.	Letters with adjacent vertical strokes need the greatest space between them.	Letters with adjacent curved or diagonal strokes need the least space.

The space needed between letters with open sides can be judged by drawing a line into the letter from which to shade in, as shown on the right.

CST

You can leave as much or as little space as you like between letters, provided the spacing looks equal.

GOODBY

GOODBYE

Ignore the *ascenders* and *descenders* when shading between small letters.

alc

Line spacing

Line spacing is the space between two consecutive lines of lettering or type.

Some designs look right with very tight line spacing, with ascenders and descenders touching.

Other designs look best with greater line spacing. Line spacing should be measured from one base line to another.

know that the vented befor he tin opener

big. it had on ead, one in its ne in its back.

osaurus had three brains, though none of them were very big. It had one

In general, the longer the line the greater the line spacing should be. Varied line spacing adds interest to lettering.

Today trip to holida deluxe ten likely year from bing sno high ma at t

Today' trip to F holiday l deluxe de With over you're likely three years What more c are over two r mornings by a amongst

Calligraphy

The word *calligraphy* comes from the Greek "kallos" meaning beautiful and "graphos" meaning writing.

Some experts claim calligraphy is a performance, like music and dancing – a skill that depends on practice and conveying feeling to look good. Others simply think of it as beautiful writing.

Many styles of calligraphy are used today, but most have their roots in old styles written with a broad nib.

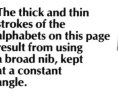

Square capitals

Ancient Roman square capitals
Square capitals, or Quadrata, were the broad pen versions of roman capitals, and were used for books and important documents. This style is considered very elegant and formal.

Rustic capitals

Ancient Roman rustic capitals
Rustic capitals were used by the Romans and are based on square capitals, but are more condensed and less formal looking. This became the main book hand.

Uncials

Uncials
Uncials developed from square capitals and were used as a book hand by the Romans and early Christians. The letters were often 1 inch high, for which the Roman name was "uncia".

Half-uncials

Half-uncial
The half-uncial were so called because they were often half an inch high. They are similar to uncials, except there are longer extensions above and below the body of the letters.

Carolingian minuscule

Carolingian minuscule
Charlemagne, king of the Franks (France and part of Germany) standardized writing with a style called Carolingian minuscule – the first small letters. He also introduced spacing between words on a regular basis.

Gothic

After minuscule hands
After Charlemagne, different versions of the minuscule were developed. One of these was called Textura, because it is so closely written that a page of it resembles woven cloth.

Italic script

Humanist scripts
New styles of writing, called Humanist scripts, were developed in Italy during the Renaissance. You can find out how to do one of these, called italic writing, over the page.

The lost art
By the late 19th century the art of writing with a broad nib was virtually lost. Handwriting was done with a pointed steel nib and thick and thin strokes made by exerting pressure.

Victorian lettering artists tried copying old styles, but most did not realize that the shape of the letters was made by the angle of a broad nib.

This style, done with a thin nib, was fashionable in the 19th century.

◀ Edward Johnston

In the 1890s Edward Johnston studied old manuscripts and re-discovered how the letterforms were written. He designed a basic alphabet, called the Foundation Hand, based on a form of writing used at Winchester in the 10th century.

Foundation Hand

Illuminated manuscripts

Many manuscripts, from medieval times and before, were beautifully decorated, or "illuminated", with patterns, pictures and elaborate borders, sometimes in gold.

Page from an illuminated manuscript.

Decorated initial letter

Many old manuscripts have decorated initial letters, like the one above. These seem to be saying, "start here", as well as adding decoration. You could use the same principle in your own lettering.

Modern calligraphy

Today, calligraphy is most often used where decorative effect is important.

Decorative alphabet

It is often used for book covers, invitations and greetings cards.

Poetry

Poems

Invitation

You are invited to a WEDDING

THE GREAT FIRE

Book cover

Have a very Happy Birthday

Greetings card

Limbering-up

Calligraphy depends upon the flow and rhythm of a pen or brush rather than being drawn. Before starting something important calligraphers often find it useful to limber-up in order to get in the right frame of mind.

Changing nib angle

Try altering the nib or brush angle to see what happens to the shape of letters.

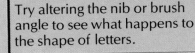

ABCDE
Horizontal

ABCDE
45°

ABCDE
90°

Contrast

DESIGN TIPS

Any message can be made more interesting to look at by including a contrast between the parts, called design elements. The pictures on the right show some of the different elements that you can contrast, either singly or together. Experiment with different combinations.

ABCDEF GHIJKLMNOPQ OPQRST
Size

ABCDEFG NOPQRS HIJKLMN
Style

ABCDE MNOPQ TUVWX
Weight

ABCDEFG HIJKLMNOPQ RSTUVW
Size & weight

HIJKLM PQRST TUVWX
Colour

BCDEF GHIJK LMNO
Position

Italic writing

In fifteenth century Italy, new styles of writing developed, including what is today called the italic hand. It is now a popular style of *calligraphy*, quick enough to be used for everyday writing.

Use the examples on these pages as a starting point. Copy them first, using guide lines (see page 3), then let a style of your own develop as you write more quickly.

Italic pens

There are lots of specially made italic pens you can buy.

Left-oblique nib

For italic writing you need a pen with a square-shaped nib. Learning is easiest with as broad a nib as you can get. If you are left-handed you may need a left-oblique nib, as shown above.

Nib angle

Hold the nib at 45° to the guide lines, keeping it at the same angle as you form the letters.

Draw a vertical cross with your pen to help get the angle right. Both parts of the cross will be the same thickness if you have the nib at 45°.

Proportions

Use the proportions shown below to draw your guide lines. Guide lines are not necessary for everyday writing, except to begin with.

Capitals
7 pen widths

Small letters

Adg 5 pen widths

Small letters

Build up your confidence by copying the small letters below in the order shown. (The alphabet is divided into groups of similar shaped letters.) Try writing individual letters over and over, then try a complete alphabet before writing words.

In italic writing letters should slant forwards slightly (about 5°).

These marks show the height of letters in pen nib widths.

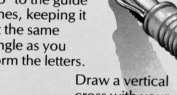

oecagbd

pqijnmhru

vwxyzslkft

Joining letters

Many letters in italic writing can be joined up to make words, so that the writing flows and can be done quickly.

The quick brown fox jumps over the lazy dog

Joined-up letters

There are two kinds of joins – diagonal and horizontal. You will find out for yourself which letters are best left unjoined, but here are a few tips:

eo

These letters can be joined from both sides.

nm

These letters are best joined from the right only.

dgqa

Avoid joining onto the left of these letters.

bp

Avoid joining onto the right of these letters.

Capitals

Capitals in italic writing are quite similar to ancient Roman capitals (see page 8). The style of the basic capital letterform can be varied a great deal by adding decorative strokes, called flourishes. Letters like this are sometimes called swash capitals.

The alphabet to copy and learn below shows a basic version of each letter (for ordinary use), along with a decorative version of it.

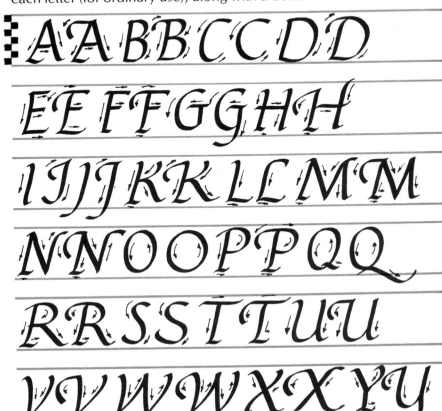

(see page 8)

Writing a letter

Here are some tips on laying out a letter.

Margin proportions

Too small   Too large   Pleasing to look at.

Alternative layouts for letter headings. ▼

Alternative layouts for envelopes. ▼

History

In fifteenth century Italy new writing styles developed, called Humanist scripts. Their capitals were influenced by Roman letters and the small letters by an earlier style called Carolingian minuscule. This was the beginning of italic writing as known today.

aenobire pm

Carolingian minuscule

Around 1523 Arrighi published a printed manual in Rome for people to copy from. His copy-book was influential throughout Europe.

Page from a printed copy-book.

Tips on spacing

Try not to pack letters too closely together as it makes words difficult to read. But beware — if the letters are too wide, the shape of the words may be lost.

| Too close | *tight* | Correct | *Spacing* |

Allow the space of a small letter "o" between words.

Word spacing

Leave a space two small "o"s high between the "x" height guide lines.

grey
deal

Script writing

Script is a term loosely applied to a number of informal writing styles often used for display purposes. There are no strict rules about how it must be done, except that it must be legible. Try copying the styles on these pages and then see if you can invent your own.

Greetings card

Have a very Happy Birthday

SALE NOW ON!

SPONSORED FUN RUN 2·00pm TODAY

Different styles of script writing

Shop sign

Poster

Pens

Any kind of pen can be used for script lettering. There are also special script pens, with round or square-shaped nibs which lay flat on the paper. These give a constant stroke thickness, needed for styles like "script *sans serif*", shown on the right.

Round-tipped felt pens also give a constant stroke thickness.

These are called "Speedball" nibs, but other makes are available.

"B" series nibs are round and keep the same weight of line.

"C" and "D" series nibs make thick and thin strokes.

"A" series nibs are square and make strokes of the same weight.

Pointed nib for fine script.

Script sans serif

aAbBcCdDeEfFgG
hHiIjJkKlLmMnN
oOpPqQrRsStTuUvV
wWxXyYzZ

Try to keep these letterforms very rounded, with short ascenders.

Informal script

abcdefgh
ijklmnopqrsstu
vwxyz3

This is based on ordinary writing, with added flourishes. Try to join the letters in a smooth, unbroken line.

Techniques

abcde

Erase line when finished.

Instead of using guide lines, draw a pencil line and write across it as shown. Script often looks best if the letters appear to "dance", but with the body of the letters kept on a constant centre line.

Where possible, make the strokes by pulling the pen towards you. For large letters, turn the paper to do this.

Retouch letters with white paint if necessary.

Rough edges corrected.

Terminals painted out to make square ends.

Brush lettering

Script letters drawn freely with a brush have a distinctive style of their own, but need lots of practice to get right.

Use a pointed watercolour brush, held so that you use its side.

The more pressure you use, the wider the stroke will be.

Practise these two strokes.

Pompeii

Roman street notices and graffiti painted by brush were found in Pompeii, in Italy, preserved by the volcanic ash which destroyed the town in 79AD.

The Romans also used a brush to sketch letters on stone before carving them.

Eastern writing

In the East, brushes have been used for thousands of years to produce beautiful calligraphy. The picture below shows part of a Chinese message.

In Chinese, each character is a single word. **Chinese is read vertically, and from right to left.**

承 们 近 书 是
祖 决 代 法 从
国 定 著 笔 他

In China, fine handwriting is seen as a mark of respect.

You can buy Chinese brushes from some art shops to use for brush lettering. The brush is held vertically, and controlled by the thumb, index and middle fingers.

This is called the Ping Wan grip. **Block of Chinese ink**

The ink is rubbed with water on a stone. **Different Chinese brushes**

Brush lettering alphabet

ABCDEFGHIJKLM
NOPQRSTUVWXYZ
1234567890

You can copy almost any style of lettering with a brush, but this one is good to practise with.

DESIGN TIPS

Cut and paste

It is often very difficult to make script lettering look right – a message may look fine overall, but be spoilt by a few characters.

You can overcome this problem by writing lots of versions and then using a technique called "cut and paste" to combine the best parts of each.

This technique is also suitable for other styles shown in this book.

1

Write your message several times, at the same size.

2

Paste the strips together as shown, taking care to get the spacing right.

3

Choose the best parts and cut them into strips.

4

Photocopy the page and, if necessary, paint out any cut marks and photocopy again.

Sketching letters

You can create letters quickly in almost any style by sketching them – either by copying an alphabet* or by learning a style. These pages show some methods for roughing out ideas for anything from a poster to a record sleeve, and for creating lively letters for finished work. Sketching also helps you to understand the shape of each letter, and forces you away from your normal handwriting style. To start with, it is a good idea to copy and learn roman capitals, shown on the opposite page.

Sketching methods

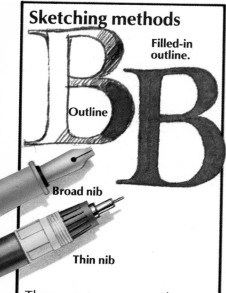

Filled-in outline.

Outline

Broad nib

Thin nib

There are two approaches to sketching letters: you can either sketch an outline and then fill it in, or use a broad nib (or similar shaped tool) to make the thickness of each letter in one go.

Sketching tools

Almost anything that makes a mark will do for sketching.

Felt pen

Carpenter's pencil

Shaped piece of balsa wood to dip in ink.

Two pencils or pens taped together are very good for sketching large letters.

Broad-pen sketching

You need to hold a broad nib pen (or similarly shaped tool) at a constant angle to make thick and thin strokes on each letter. The angle varies from style to style, but for upright capitals, like those on the opposite page, you need to hold the pen at between 30°-45° to the horizontal.

1
Hold the pen as shown below.

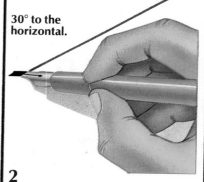

30° to the horizontal.

2
Keep your hand and the nib at the same angle while you form the letter.

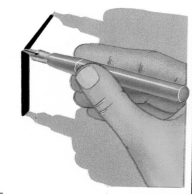

Try to move your hand with a smooth, flowing action.

Outline method

Series of short, slightly curved strokes.

By keeping your hand stationary on the paper and using the natural movement of your fingers, you can sketch outline letters like those above. You can then fill in the outline if you prefer.

1
Keep your hand still and move your fingers as shown below to make horizontal or vertical strokes.

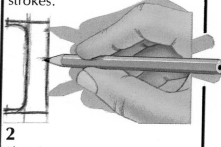

2
Sketch rounded strokes by moving your fingers as shown below.

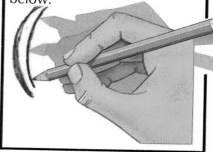

*There are alphabets to copy on pages 40-46.

Adding serifs

You can finish your letters by adding *serifs* with a pointed pen or pencil as shown below.

Imagine circles forming the outline of serifs, as shown below.

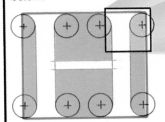

Serifs should be about a quarter of the circle and should appear to grow out of the stem of the letter.

Guide lines

Before sketching letters in any style, it helps to draw guide lines on your paper to help get the correct proportion of height to width of each letter.

1 For roman capitals, guide lines should be about nine times the thickest part of the letter.

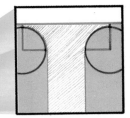

2 If you are using a pen, measure the height by marking with the nib like this.

Roman capitals

The letters shown below are grouped according to their shape. Sketch each stroke slowly and deliberately, in the order shown by the arrows. It is a good idea to practise with a phrase like "The quick brown fox jumps over the lazy dog", as it includes all the letters of the alphabet.

Square graph paper is useful for sketching, as the squares help to get the letters in proportion.

All curved letters overlap the guide lines slightly, top and bottom. This makes these letters look as though they line up properly with others in a word – the result of an optical illusion.

The upper parts of an S and B are slightly larger than the lower parts.

Balance

All the parts of a well-designed layout should balance. You can get a layout to balance either symmetrically or asymmetrically. A symmetrical layout is said to balance when there is an even distribution of visual weight on each side of its horizontal and vertical axis. Visual weight is not something you can measure, but something you have to see.

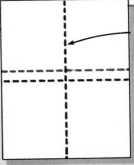

The vertical axis is an imaginary line down the middle.

The position of this line will depend on the visual impact of the words above and below it.

The true horizontal axis is an imaginary line across the centre. Because of an optical illusion, a line above this is the one used to balance the layout.

A symmetrical and an asymmetrical layout are shown below. In general, symmetrical layouts are easier to handle.

Symmetrical layout

Asymmetrical layout

You can use either approach in anything you design.

Drawn lettering

Lettering can be carefully drawn or painted, rather than being written directly with a pen. There are four main stages involved, explained on these pages. You may find the alphabets on pages 40-46 helpful if you want a style to copy.

1st stage — Pencil rough

There are several ways of drawing the basic outline: by construction, sketching or tracing.

Construction

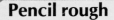

There is an alphabet like this to copy on page 44.

Letterforms can be carefully measured and lightly drawn out in pencil using a T-square and set square.

Sketching

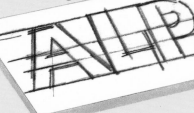

Sketch the style you want, as explained on pages 16-17.

Tracing

Trace the letters you want from an alphabet, then enlarge or reduce them using one of the methods shown on page 39.

2nd stage — Filling in

Fill in the outline with colour or black ink. Some examples are shown below.

"Hatched" crayon lines.

Felt pen

Waterproof black ink is best if you want to reproduce the lettering by photocopying or some other method.

When using a brush, don't take the ink (or paint) right up to the edge of the letters until the third stage.

Paint

Use a pointed brush.

3rd stage — Outline

Next you may need to finish the outline, smoothing the edges and removing any unevenness left from the previous stage.

When drawing geometrical letterforms a ruling pen, used with a ruler as a guide, is good for crisp ink lines. These are quite difficult to use, so you need to practise beforehand.

Technical pen

You could draw outlines freehand, especially for curved parts.

Be careful when using Indian ink as it takes several minutes to dry.

Run the metal part of the brush along the ruler.

A fine brush is a good tool for finishing outlines, with a ruler as a guide, tipped back a little as shown.

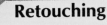

Retouching

Use white paint* and a fine brush to tidy up any imperfections. This is called retouching. If your work is for reproduction (printing or photocopying), any retouched parts will not show when printed.

You may need to do a lot of retouching if you draw the outline freehand.

Drawing curved parts

The drawing instruments shown below are useful aids for drawing curved parts of letterforms.

French curves

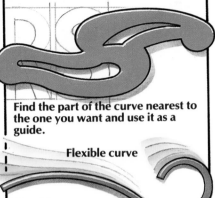

Find the part of the curve nearest to the one you want and use it as a guide.

Flexible curve

Bend the curve to the shape you want.

Constructing serifs

For roman lettering, *serifs* can be constructed using a pair of compasses, as shown below.

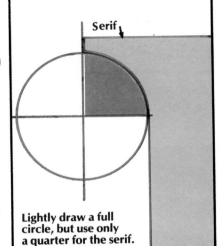

Serif

Lightly draw a full circle, but use only a quarter for the serif.

Drawing "straight" parts

The stems of many letterforms curve inwards slightly. An optical illusion actually makes them look straight. You will need to take this into account when drawing most non-geometric letters.

A B
abc

The typeface used in this book, called Optima, has curved stems as a deliberate effect.

You could use a ruler as a guide and tilt the pen as you draw to make a slight curve.

2 When drawing freehand, first draw a straight pencil outline, then use this as a guide for drawing a slight curve.

Spacing

Here is how to work out the length of lines of lettering to fit in a certain space.

1 At the sketch stage, sketch the lettering in lines, the width of your paper. Then cut the lettering into strips.

Paste the strips **2** onto a piece of paper, in the position you want them.

3 Trace off the lettering onto another piece of paper, ready for rendering.

DESIGN TIPS

Tracing

Designers often make a series of tracings of a drawing, improving each one bit by bit as they go.

1

Start with a sketch.

2

Place tracing paper over the sketch and trace over it, improving the parts you don't like and keeping the parts you do.

3

Continue using the last drawing to trace from, until you have a perfect copy.

Special paint called process white is available for this.

Special effects

There are many ways of distorting letters to create special effects. For example, you can make lettering work both as a word and as a picture of the word, like this: SWITCHBACK

Some ideas are shown here, but you can probably think of more.

Draw the words in black ink on a piece of paper.

Crumple the paper, open it out, and take a photocopy of it.

Trace the lettering from the photocopy, enlarging it if needed.*

Carefully render the finished tracing with ink or paint.

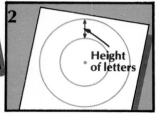

Draw the words between guide lines on a piece of paper.

With a pair of compasses, draw two circles as shown.

Mark where each letter goes when the spacing looks right.

Cut up the letters and lay them around the circle.

Lightly glue the letters, then trace them. Render the finished letters.

Perspective

There are two main ways of drawing letters in perspective, to give the illusion of depth: single and two-point. Both methods are explained here.

You can create good effects by pasting perspective lettering over backgrounds from magazines.

Single-point perspective

Use this method to make letters appear to be facing you in 3-D.

1 Draw parallel guide lines (A and B) and then the letters.

2 Mark a "vanishing point".

The lower the vanishing point, the more you appear to look up at the lettering.

The higher the vanishing point, the more you appear to look down.

5 Draw the outline and colour or ink in the letters.

4 Lightly join all points on the letters to the vanishing point.

3 Draw two lines (C and D) parallel to the guide lines, the depth you want the letters.

Shadow letters

1 Draw parallel guide lines, shown in red. Draw the lettering as an outline between the top two.

2 Trace the lettering and superimpose it over the first outline, to line up with the bottom guide line.

3 Ink or colour in the sides of the letters, as shown in blue.

4 Draw in the pencil outlines in ink.

Distorted letters

1 Draw the letters, with a grid over them, as shown.

2 Draw a distorted grid freehand and sketch the letters to occupy the same proportion of each square of the grid.

3 Trace the sketch and fill in with ink or paint.

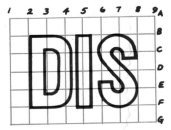

Number and letter the grid.

Number in the same way as the first grid.

Reversed

Draw or trace the letters in pencil as an outline.

DIS | RE

Ink or colour in the background.

Two-point perspective

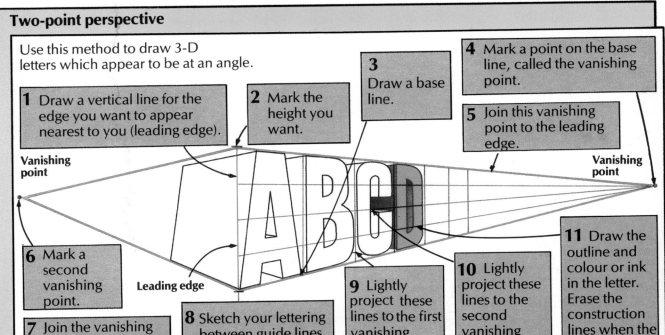

Use this method to draw 3-D letters which appear to be at an angle.

1 Draw a vertical line for the edge you want to appear nearest to you (leading edge).

2 Mark the height you want.

3 Draw a base line.

4 Mark a point on the base line, called the vanishing point.

5 Join this vanishing point to the leading edge.

6 Mark a second vanishing point.

7 Join the vanishing point to the leading edge.

8 Sketch your lettering between guide lines here.

9 Lightly project these lines to the first vanishing point.

10 Lightly project these lines to the second vanishing point.

11 Draw the outline and colour or ink in the letter. Erase the construction lines when the ink is dry.

Vanishing point

Vanishing point

Leading edge

3-D lettering

3-D letters are those with a raised or lowered surface and are used for signs, numbers, displays and so on. This page explains how to cut letters from different materials, such as card, polystyrene, wood, plaster and lino.

Card

You can make quite thick letters from corrugated card by gluing several pieces together. This process is called laminating.

1 Draw letters the size you want and trace onto corrugated card with carbon paper.

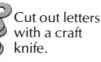
Card

2 Repeat step 1 so there are enough pieces of card to make letters the thickness you want.

3 Cut out letters with a craft knife.

4 Glue on.
Glue, or laminate, letters together.

5 Fill the edges with Polyfilla*.

6 When dry, sandpaper and paint the edges.

7 Mount the letters on a backboard or stand.

Polystyrene

3-D letters can be made very quickly from polystyrene.

1 Carbon paper
Draw letters the size you want and trace them onto polystyrene with carbon paper.

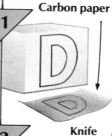

2 Knife
Cut around letters with a sharp knife using a sawing action.

Hot wire cutter
You can get special hot wire cutters which cut polystyrene very quickly and cleanly, but are expensive.

3 Paint the letters. Spray paint is ideal, but test a scrap first in case it melts the polystyrene.

4 Mount the letters on a backboard or base.

Glue

Wood

Use solid timber or marine plywood for permanent outdoor letters. Medium density fibreboard is ideal for indoors and is easy to cut.

1 Draw letters the size you want and trace them onto the wood with carbon paper.

2 Cut round letters with a jig saw, fret saw or band saw.

Jig saw	Fret saw	Band saw

3 To cut out the middle of letters, first drill a hole as shown, large enough to take the saw blade.

4 Finish letters by sanding and then polishing, varnishing or painting.

You may need screw holes to fix letters to a wall.

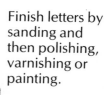

22

Trade name for decorating filler.

Carving letters

There are two kinds of carving – relief and incised. Relief letters are raised above the surface of the material; incised letters are cut into it.

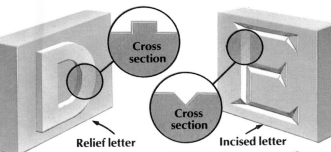

Cross section

Cross section

Relief letter

Incised letter

Lettering has been incised into many different materials since Palaeolithic times. The ancient Romans are considered by many experts to have produced the most beautiful stone inscriptions of all time.

Roman inscription

Materials

There are many materials you can use for carving: clay, stone, wood, plaster, lino – even chocolate.

For stone you need to buy proper chisels, but for softer materials you can use ordinary wood chisels and knives.

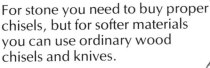

Lighting effects

DESIGN TIPS

You can alter the appearance of any 3-D lettering by lighting it differently.

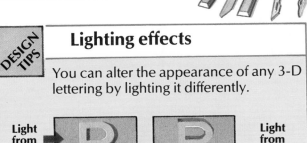

Light from the side.

Light from below.

Light from above.

Light from an angle.

Relief carving

Lino (from an art shop) is good for practising relief carving.

Draw the letters and transfer them to the lino with carbon paper.

Using lino cutters, gradually cut the material, working away from the edge of the letter.

Always work away from your fingers and eyes.

Finished lino-cut.

Incised letters

A block of plaster of Paris is good for practising incised lettering. You need a chisel and mallet.

Mallet

Chisel

Add plaster (about 5kg) to half a bowl of water until it forms a peak just above the surface. Mix thoroughly with the flat of your hand.

When hard, tip the plaster block out of the bowl.

1 Draw the letters and transfer them to the surface with carbon paper.

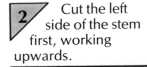

2 Cut the left side of the stem first, working upwards.

The aim is to form a "V".

Lightly tap the chisel.

3 Then cut the right side of the stem.

4 Cut the inside of curves first, starting near the narrowest part of the letter.

Cut serifs after this, if the style includes them.

Finished carving

Other ways of making letters

Stencilling

Stencilled lettering is used mainly for functional purposes – labelling crates, for example – but it can also be used decoratively. There are two kinds of stencil: those you buy and those you make.

Stencilled crate

The letters in a stencil are reproduced by painting or drawing through the holes.

These parts, called bridges, prevent the letters from falling apart.

Making a stencil

1 Draw the lettering you want and glue it to a piece of card. This is called a cutting key.

2 Place a piece of stencil paper over the lettering and tape it down. Stencil paper is waxed, making it water resistant for painting.

Stencil paper

3 Cut through the paper, along the outline of each letter. Keep the blade at an angle to make an undercut so paint does not bleed under the stencil.

Blade must be sharp.

Cut each line in a single stroke.

Undercut

4 Either draw, spray or brush paint through the stencil. Be careful not to smudge the lettering when you lift the stencil.

Use a stiff brush like this.

Keep brush upright and dab it up and down.

Blunt end

For much larger lettering you could cut a stencil from cardboard.

There is a specially designed stencil alphabet to copy and use on page 40.

Cut paper lettering

Many famous artists have used cut coloured paper to make lettering, especially on collages. You can make collages by gluing lettering cut from coloured paper to a plain background.

How to cut letters

There are two ways of cutting letters, shown below.

1

This produces uneven, but lively letters.

Fix in your mind an idea of the shape you want and cut directly into the paper.

2 Draw the letters you want onto coloured paper and cut them out with a scalpel.

Another way of making letters from coloured paper is to cut strips and glue them edge on, as shown below.

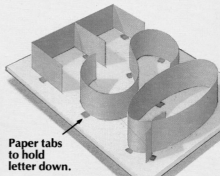

Paper tabs to hold letter down.

Rubbings

You can take rubbings on paper with wax crayon from any relief or incised lettering – manhole covers, coins, signs, inscriptions and so on.

Examples of rubbings.

1 Place the paper over the surface and rub with the crayon edge.

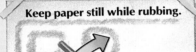

Keep paper still while rubbing.

Crayon

2 **Different colour wax crayons.**

An unusual way of lettering is to build up a library of rubbings, then cut them into individual letters to make alphabets.

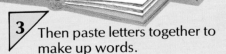

3 Then paste letters together to make up words.

Spraying

Spray painting (or airbrushing) is a good way of creating fade effects like this.

Professional illustrators use an airbrush to create "chrome" effects like this.

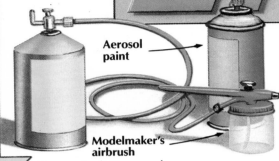

Aerosol paint

Modelmaker's airbrush

You can spray fade effects with cheap aerosol spray paints or modelmaker's airbrushes.

1 Draw the letters and trace them onto the surface you want to spray.

2 Stick masking film* over the letters and carefully cut round the outline without cutting the surface. You could cut a stencil instead, but masking film gives a better edge because the ink or paint is less likely to "bleed" under it.

Masking film

3 Spray the lightest colour first, keeping your hand moving while spraying. Let the colour dry.

4 Lightly spray the darker colour along the bottom edge as shown.

5 When the colour is dry, remove the masking film.

*A thin plastic film, available from art shops, which sticks to the surface without damaging it when removed.

25

Typography

Typography has to do with organizing messages using, among other things, prefabricated characters. Originally typography was to do with printing, but it now applies to electronic methods of communication as well.

There have been many methods of making and setting (arranging) type, from metal through to the latest techniques using computers. All involve the use of standard, interchangeable characters.

Over the next six pages there are tips on using and getting type set. You can also find out how to identify different *typefaces* and how to use do-it-yourself type.

Hand set type. Each character to be printed used to be assembled by hand.

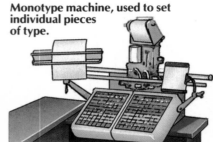

Monotype machine, used to set individual pieces of type.

Machine set type. In the 1880s Otto Mergenthaler developed a machine which set an entire line of type in molten metal.

Set of characters for phototypesetting.

Phototypesetting. In the last half century various machines have been invented which set type photographically onto paper. Later models incorporate computers.

The *copy* (words and other characters) is typed on a keyboard.

Copy can be corrected (edited) on the screen.

Digital typesetting. In the latest computer systems, characters are stored as digital codes. These are decoded and reproduced by computer-controlled laser onto photographic paper.

How to identify typefaces

There are so many typefaces that it is difficult to tell them apart. The one letter that usually gives away a typeface's identity is a small "g". Below are the "g"s of some popular typefaces.

g Baskerville	*g* Garamond	**g** Eras	g Melior	g Bookman	*g* Bodoni
g Gill Sans	**g** Souvenir	g Plantin	**g** Helvetica	**g** Univers	*g* Perpetua
g Times roman	g Caslon Old Face	*g* Century Schoolbook	**g** Futura	**g** Rockwell	g Optima

Typefaces and type designers

Some typefaces in use today were designed over four hundred yeas ago. Others are very recent. Thousands of typefaces exist and more are being designed all the time. Here are some famous typefaces and their designers.

Caslon Old Face. Designed by William Caslon, 18th C.

abcdefghijklmnopqrstuv
ABCDEFGHIJKLMN
1234567890 123456789

Until this design, the best typefaces in England were imported from Holland.

Optima. Designed by Hermann Zapf, 1958.
Zapf based his design on ancient sans serif letters.

abcdefghijklmnopqrs
ABCDEFGHIJKLMNO
1234567890 1234567890

Optima is used in different sizes and weights for the text of this book.

Univers. Designed by Adrian Frutiger, 1950s.
Univers is a family of typefaces of different weights and widths.

abcdefghijklmnopqr
ABCDEFGHIJKLMN
1234567890 .,;:'"«»&

Univers met a demand for a new sans serif typeface.

Perpetua. Designed by Eric Gill, 1920s.
Gill named his design after a female saint, martyred in AD 203.

abcdefghijklmnopqrstuvwxy
ABCDEFGHIJKLMNOPQR
1234567890 1234567890 .,;:'

This typeface was designed for the Monotype Corporation.

Bodoni. Based on types designed by Bodoni, late 18th C.

abcdefghijklmnopqrstu
ABCDEFGHIJKLMN
1234567890 123456789

This is a "modern" typeface because of its strong contrasts of thicks and thins and its hair-line serifs.

Garamond. Designed by Jean Jannon, 17th C.
Garamonds are still popular typefaces today.

abcdefghijklmnopqrst
ABCDEFGHIJKLMNO
1234567890 .,;:'"«»&!?

Called Garamond because it was thought to have been designed by him.

Futura. Designed by Paul Renner, 1928.
Futura is based on geometric shapes, repeated through the alphabet.

abcdefghijklmnopqrs
ABCDEFGHIJKLMN
1234567890 .,;:'"«»&

This typeface reflects the ideas of the modern movement in design of the period.

Other alphabets

Alphabets other than roman are also typeset. Below are four other alphabets and how to pronounce their letters.

Greek 24 letters

α	Alpha	π	Pi
β	Beta	ρ	Rho
γ	Gamma	σ	Sigma
δ	Delta	τ	Tau
ε	Epsilon	υ	Upsilon
ζ	Zeta	φ	Phi
θ	Eta	χ	Chi
θ	Theta	ψ	Psi
ι	Iota	ω	Omega
κ	Kappa		
λ	Lamda		
μ	Mu		
ν	Nu		
ξ	Xi		
o	Omicron		

Cyrillic (used in Russia) 33 letters

А а	Ah	Ии	Ee
Б б	Beh	Йй	E kratkoe
В в	Veh	К к	Kah
Г г	Geh	Лл	El
Д д	Deh	М м	Em
Е е	Eh	Н н	En
Ё ё	Yo	О о	O
Ж ж	Zheh	П п	Peh
З з	Zeh	Р р	Er
		С с	Ess
		Т т	Teh
		У у	Oo
Ф ф	Ef		
Х х	Kha		
Ц ц	Tseh		
Ч ч	Cheh		
Ш ш	Shah		
Щ щ	Shchah		
ъ ъ	Tverdi znak		
ы ы	Yeri		
ь ь	Myarki znak		
Э э	Eh		
Ю ю	Yoo		
Я я	Yah		

Hebrew 26 letters

א	Alef	ו	Vav	ס	Samekh
ב	Bet	ז	Zayin	ע	Ayin
ב	Vet	ח	Chet	פ	Pe
ג	Gimmel	ט	Tet	פ	Fe
ד	Dalet	י	Yod	צ	Tzade
ה	He	כ	Kaf	ק	Kof
		כ	Khaf	ר	Resh
		ל	Lamed	ש	Shin
		מ	Mem	ש	Sin
		נ	Nun	ת	Tav/Taw

Arabic 28 letters

ا	Hamzah		Dhal		Ghayn
	Ba		Ra		Fa
	Ta		Za		Qaf
	Tha		Sin		Faf
	Jim		Shin		Lam
	Ha		Sad		Mim
	Kha		Dad		Nun
	Dal		Ta		Ha
			Za		Waw
			'ayn		Ya

Numbers

There are two main kinds of numbers, shown below.

1234567890

◄ Old style (or non-ranging). The 3, 4, 5, 7 and 9 drop below the base line. The 6 and 8 extend above it.

Modern (or ranging). All the numbers line up between two lines. These look better with modern type styles. ►

1234567890

27

Using type

These pages explain the typographical terms you need to know to turn *copy* (hand or typewritten words) into *typesetting*.

Measuring type

Three important measurements are used in typesetting. They are shown on the right with the special units used to measure them.

1 Height of the body of the type, called the type size (measured in points but sometimes in millimetres).

2 The distance between one line of type and another (measured from baseline to baseline in points or millimetres).

Making pots on a potter's wheel is called "throwing". The name describes how the clay is thrown outwards by the force of the rotating wheel. By controlling this force you can make a huge range of shapes.

3 Column width, called the line length or measure (measured in picas or millimetres).

Type size

Two systems are used to measure type: the Anglo-American *point* (English speaking countries), and the *Didot* point (Europe). The Didot point is slightly larger than the Anglo-American point.

Millimetres are also used, but usually only for large sizes.

Anglo-American point

12 points = 1 pica
1 point = approx. 1/72in
1 pica   12×1/72in = 1/6in.

72pt

Size of type in points.

The size of type is usually expressed in points.

The Didot point

12 points = 1 cicero
1 point = 0.376mm
1 cicero = 4.5111mm

72pt

Size of type in points.

The x-height

Different type styles, all of the same point size, may look large or small when compared with one another. This is because their *x-heights* are not the same.

Garamond   Times roman

X   X

30pt type   30pt type

Line feed

Line feed is the distance between one line of type and another, measured from baseline to baseline. It used to be called leading, when a strip of metal was inserted between lines of type to make a gap.

Type can be set closely or with additional line feed.

Closely set lines of type.

had a little lamb
eece was white as snow
verywhere that Mary went

had a little lamb
eece was white as snow
verywhere that Mary went

Lines with 2 point extra line feed.

Calculating depth

Special "rulers" called *depth scales* are used to calculate the depth of type of different sizes.

This example shows how to work out the depth of a column of 6 lines of type of a certain size.

10/12pt type (said as, "10 on 12 point"). This means 10pt type on a 12pt line feed.

Ignore the type size – use the bottom figure as it gives the line feed. Using the 12 point scale, mark where shown.

Each column represents one size of type.

This is the depth of 6 lines of any typeface set on 12pt lines.

Other sizes are marked on the back.

Type set with the size of the type the same as the line feed is written like this

Depth scale

Line lengths

Type is set in two main ways: *justified* and *unjustified*.

Justified type	Unjustified type
Hey diddle diddle the cat had a fiddle the cow jumped over the moon	Hey diddle diddle the cat had a fiddle the cow jumped over the moon

The line length is the maximum width, called the measure, of a line of type. It is measured in picas, *ciceros*, or millimetres (see below).

You can use the 12pt part of a depth scale to measure type widthways. This is because 12 points = 1 pica/cicero.

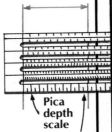

Pica depth scale

This example shows the width of 10 picas of any size of type.

Marking up

Marking up means writing instructions on your copy for the typesetter to follow. Special codes are used in the margin, as shown in the chart below.

ital	Italics
bf	Bold
cap	Capitals
¶	New paragraph
#	Insert space
⌒	Close up gap
⊐	Move type to the right
⊏	Move type to the left
trs	Transpose words
no ¶	Run on (no new paragraph)
☞	Delete (remove)
/	Insert new words

Here is an example of marked-up copy.

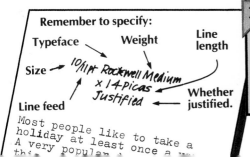

Remember to specify:

Typeface   Weight   Line length

Size → 10/11pt Rockwell Medium x 14 Picas Justified

Line feed   Whether justified.

Most people like to take a holiday at least once a...
A very popular...

Ems

An em is a square the size of a typeface's point size.

12pts — 12pt em — 12pts

36pts — 36pt em — 36pts

A 12 point em is often used as a measurement of width, since a 12 point em is the same width as 1 pica.

12pt em ■ = 1 pica ■

Copy fitting

Copy fitting (or casting off) means calculating how much space copy will occupy when typeset in a certain typeface and size. This example shows one method of copy fitting.

Typewritten copy

Once upon a time there was an aard called Androcles, lived in an enorm palace, where he spent most of his the sun. Sadly there were no ot aardvarks around company, so poor Androcles was qui lonely.

Once upon a time aardvark called A an enormous pala

Same copy in 10/11pt

Once upon a time there wa lived in an enormous palac lazing around in the sun. Sa around for compa...

Same copy in 6/7pt

1 Find the total number of characters by multiplying the average number per line by the number of lines of text.

Count spaces and punctuation marks as characters.

there was an aardva called Androcles. lived in an enormou palace, w **243 characters**

2 Decide on the measure (width) you want to use.

8 PICAS
10 PICAS
12 PICAS

This grid has columns 13 picas wide.

3 Decide on the typeface and size.

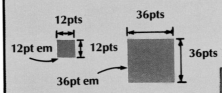

10/11pt Eras

abcdefghijklmnopqrstu
ABCDEFGHIJKLMNO
1234567890 .,;:'" «»&!?

4 Divide the total number of characters in the text by the number of characters per line. Typesetters supply specimen sheets with tables showing characters per pica for sizes of type.

Point size	Width of column					
Picas	10	11	12	13	14	15
8pt	31	35	39	43	47	51
9pt	30	33	36	39	42	45
10pt	29	31	33	35	37	39

Number of characters

37 characters in 14 picas

$243 \div 37 = 6.56$ lines

5 Round up to the nearest whole number and mark off the depth with a depth scale.

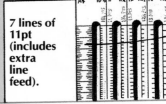

7 lines of 11pt (includes extra line feed).

If the typesetting comes out too long, start again with:

*A smaller type size, or
*Wider columns, or
*Smaller line feed, or
*Less copy

If the typesetting is too short, try:

*A larger type size, or
*Narrower columns, or
*Greater line feed, or
*Add pictures, or
*Leave spaces

Designing with type

This page gives some tips on things to take into account when designing with type.

Display and text type

Typefaces are designed for two different uses: those for large blocks of *copy* are called text, or book, faces; those for headings and titles are called display faces.

Display faces

CHARMMA

COMPASS

Bloody Horror

SLIPSTREAM

Many more display faces have been designed than text faces.

Display faces are usually 14 points or larger.

Text faces

Optima

Times

Univers

Baskerville

Text faces are sometimes used for headings too, as in this book.

Impact

Headings have most impact when set with the first letter as a capital and the rest as small letters. Capitals join visually top and bottom.

Man eating monster feels ill

MAN EATING MONSTER FEELS ILL

Size

Choose a type size appropriate to your message and audience. The further away the message is to be read, the larger the typeface must be, for example.

Beware of the drop

Once upon a time

Type weight

The boldness of a typeface is called its weight.

Eras light

Eras book

Eras medium

Eras semi bold

Eras bold

For text, it is usually best not to use too bold a typeface.

Legibility

Legibility means how easy or difficult something is to read. There are many things that affect legibilty; some are explained below.

- *Sans serif* is thought to be less easy to read than *serif* type. This may be because some sans serif letters look more similar to one another than letters with serifs do, unlike those with serifs. ▶

  I must go down to the sea again, to the lonely sea and the sky, I left my shoes and socks there, I wonder if they're dry?
  Serif

  I must go down to the sea again, to the lonely sea and the sky, I left my shoes and socks there, I wonder if they're dry ?
  Sans serif

- Large areas of text set in capitals takes longer to read than those set in small letters. ▶

  Lucy Legwarmer, aged 8, was first on the scene when her dog Spike pinned the burglar against the wall.

  LUCY LEGWARMER, AGED 8, WAS FIRST ON THE SCENE WHEN HER DOG SPIKE PINNED THE BURGLAR AGAINST THE WALL.

- Very short and very long lines of type are hard to read. ▼

Very few people realize how difficult it is to parachute onto the top of a skyscraper.

Very few people realize how difficult it is to parachute onto the top of a skyscraper.

- It is best to choose only one or two type styles for a design, but to have some variation in type weight. ▶

For Sale

Turbo-powered Spacecraft.

Hardly used. Good fuel consumption. Complete with instructions. Phone 456739

Do-it-yourself type

You can do your own "typesetting" with instant lettering, typewriters and word processors.

Rub-down lettering

Instant rub-down lettering is ideal for headings and short messages.

Sheet of rub-down lettering.

1 Draw in light blue if the lettering is for printing.

Guide line

Spacing marks

Draw two guide lines: one where you want the lettering, the other in line with the space marks on the sheet.

2 Rub down space mark too.

Special tool or blunt end of pencil.

Remove the backing sheet and align the spacing marks below the letter you want on the lower blue line. Rub the letter with a tool until it appears grey.

3 Align the mark below the next letter so that it butts up against the first mark. Rub down both letter and mark.

4 You can also use masking tape to remove mistakes.

Carefully remove all the spacing marks by lifting them with a piece of masking tape.

5 Place the backing sheet over the lettering and fix them in place by rubbing with a tool.

6 Repair any damaged letters with a black pen.

7 If necessary, cut the lettering and paste it into position on your layout.

FOR SALE

Layout

Word processors

Most word processors give a choice between printing justified or unjustified text. The quality of printers varies enormously.

Printout from a poor quality printer.

Printout from a good quality printer.

Typewriters

Typewritten copy can be made to look good enough for printing, especially if you use a carbon ribbon rather than an ordinary cotton one.

Cotton ribbon ABCDE

Carbon ribbon ABCDE

You can create *justified* text with an ordinary typewriter like this:

1 Set the tab* to give the number of characters you want across a column.

2 Type the copy, with stars to fill up the end of each line.

```
Many years ago in a*
damp and smelly cave
in the woods, there*
lived a sad old*****
goblin called Fred.*
```

3 Re-type the copy with extra spaces between the words to take up the number of spaces at the end of each line.

```
Many   years ago in a
damp and smelly cave
in the   woods, there
lived    a   sad old
goblin   called Fred.
```

Typewritten copy looks best reduced by 15%-25%, as this makes some of the irregularities in the spacing less obvious.

Reduced typewritten copy

*This sets the length of a line of typing.

Page design

Any printed or written message, from books and magazines to exhibition panels and advertisements, needs to be organized in some way. This is popularly called *layout*. Good layout is the result of careful arrangement of all *graphic elements* in a message.

This page explains the technical words used to describe the layout of a magazine. The same applies to any kind of message, but not all the features shown need be used. You can also find out about layout design techniques.

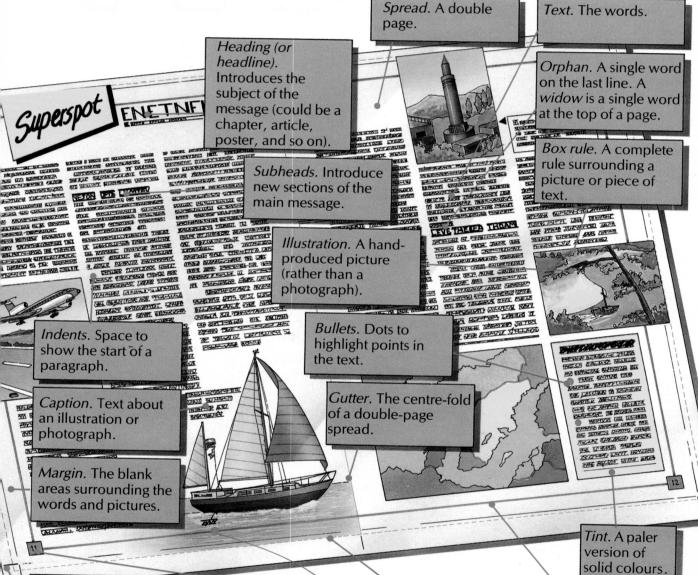

Spread. A double page.

Text. The words.

Heading (or headline). Introduces the subject of the message (could be a chapter, article, poster, and so on).

Orphan. A single word on the last line. A *widow* is a single word at the top of a page.

Box rule. A complete rule surrounding a picture or piece of text.

Subheads. Introduce new sections of the main message.

Illustration. A hand-produced picture (rather than a photograph).

Indents. Space to show the start of a paragraph.

Bullets. Dots to highlight points in the text.

Caption. Text about an illustration or photograph.

Gutter. The centre-fold of a double-page spread.

Margin. The blank areas surrounding the words and pictures.

Tint. A paler version of solid colours.

Trim or crop marks. Marks outside the page showing where the paper is to be cut.

Folio. Page number.

Label. A very short caption, often with an arrow.

Bleed. Where an illustration or photograph goes over the outside margin and off the edge of the page.

Rules. Horizontal and vertical lines, often used to divide up parts of the message.

Grids

A *grid* is like an invisible framework within which pages of books, magazines and so on are designed.

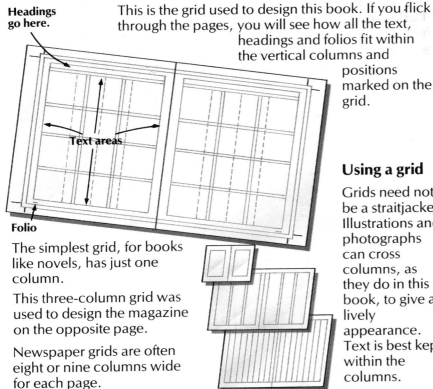

Headings go here.

This is the grid used to design this book. If you flick through the pages, you will see how all the text, headings and folios fit within the vertical columns and positions marked on the grid.

Text areas

Folio

The simplest grid, for books like novels, has just one column.

This three-column grid was used to design the magazine on the opposite page.

Newspaper grids are often eight or nine columns wide for each page.

Drawing a grid

If you want to design a magazine, comic or something similar, it is a good idea to draw a grid first.

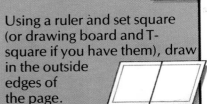

Decide on the size, or format, you need.

Using a ruler and set square (or drawing board and T-square if you have them), draw in the outside edges of the page.

Use a light blue pencil as this will not show if the page is copied for printing.

Draw in the columns and any other guide lines needed.

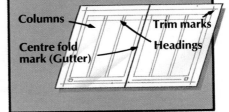

Columns   **Trim marks**

Centre fold mark (Gutter)   **Headings**

Using a grid

Grids need not be a straitjacket. Illustrations and photographs can cross columns, as they do in this book, to give a lively appearance. Text is best kept within the columns.

Electronic page layout

Some design studios use computers to design layouts. A design idea is gradually built up on the screen using the real text and pictures.

Printer

Electronic page layout software is available for many home computers.

DESIGN TIPS

Drawing layouts

Grids are essential for drawing layouts, as they help you to decide where to put things.*

Layout paper

Grid

▲ Slip your grid under tracing or layout paper to sketch ideas for a layout.

Use your best sketch to refine your ideas by tracing over it. Continue this process until the layout is ready to draw neatly.

▼ **Professional designers use this technique.**

Felt pens and markers are good for layouts.

Sketch

*See pages 26-27 to find out how to work out how much space type will occupy.

Designing an alphabet

These pages show how Michael Harvey, a well-known lettering designer, created an alphabet for this book.*

Designers go through several stages when designing a new alphabet, and you can see these at work here.

Stage 1 / Brief

Designers usually work to a brief – instructions setting out what the customer, or client, wants.

The brief here was to design a multi-purpose stencil alphabet, and to suggest some possible uses.

Stage 2 / Ideas and inspiration

Designers get their ideas from many sources – often by adapting an existing idea – and many keep files and sketch books of reference material that might be useful.

Breaks

Design briefs usually impose constraints of some kind. For example, a stencil has to have bridges in the letterforms or it will fall apart. Constraints like this help the designer to decide what to do.

ABCDEFGH IJKLMNOP QRSTUVW XYZ &?!,. Egyptian

Inspiration for the alphabet came from looking at road markings, and also at a 19th century letterform, called Egyptian. Stencil letters are often based on bold styles with heavy *serifs*.

Stage 3 / Try-outs

Next, the designer made a series of sketches to develop his ideas.

Idea 1

Drawn letter, based closely on the original Egyptian.

Idea 2

Freehand drawing, with shaped strokes and fewer serifs.

Idea 3 — The designer decided to try combining written letterforms with the original Egyptian style to make it look more elegant.

Each letter was built up, stroke by stroke, with a broad pen.

This is how it looked.

WX

ABCDEFGHIJKLM
NOPQRSTUVWXYZ

The letters were then drawn freehand, removing the lower serifs to improve the way they fit together.

See page 40.

Stage 4 / Master drawings

Master drawings, from which copies can be taken, are carefully drawn in outline on a large scale, using drawing instruments.

All parts of the letters – stems, serifs, curves – must be consistent in weight and detail from letter to letter. The letters must be drawn to work well together in any arrangement of words.

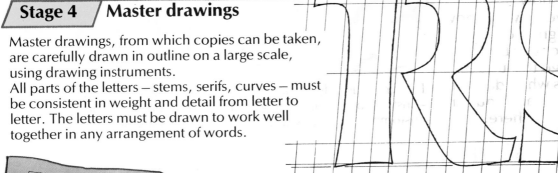

The complete alphabet drawn in outline.

At this stage, the alphabet can be enlarged or reduced photographically. A process called PMT (photo mechanical transfer) is often used to do this*.

Stage 5 / Stencils and uses

Michael Harvey suggested two uses for the alphabet: to make a road marking for a private parking space and for stencilling children's wooden alphabet blocks.

Alphabet enlarged and traced onto cardboard for a road-marking stencil.

White paint for outside use.

Alphabet traced onto waxed stencil paper to make wooden alphabet blocks.

DESIGN TIPS / Designing alphabets

Here are some points to take into account if you want to design your own alphabet.

*Parts of letters, like serifs and stems, should normally look the same for every letter in the alphabet.

*It is easier to keep details consistent if you work on groups of similar shaped letters, rather than go from A-Z.

```
IHTLEF
AVWYX
KMNZ
OQCGDUJ
PRBS
Lhnmrut
VNyxkz
ocedqpb
agsfij
```

*All letters must be either upright or slanted at the same angle.

*You can get PMTs at instant print shops.

Designing a message

Messages should be designed so as to communicate successfully their content.

These pages give tips on planning a message. To do this you first need to think about the following:

- its purpose,
- the people for whom it is intended,
- how it will be used,
- the reproduction facilities at your disposal.

The chart below shows the main kinds of messages and suggests how you might approach them.

News

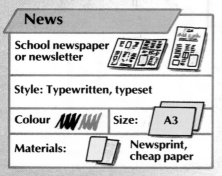

School newspaper or newsletter

Style: Typewritten, typeset

Colour		Size:	A3

Materials: Newsprint, cheap paper

Instruction

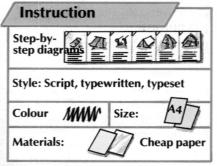

Step-by-step diagrams

Style: Script, typewritten, typeset

Colour		Size:	A4

Materials: Cheap paper

Information

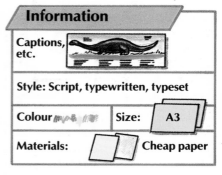

Captions, etc.

Style: Script, typewritten, typeset

Colour		Size:	A3

Materials: Cheap paper

Display

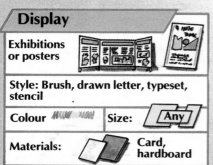

Exhibitions or posters

Style: Brush, drawn letter, typeset, stencil

Colour		Size:	Any

Materials: Card, hardboard

Advertisement

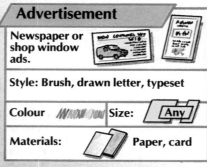

Newspaper or shop window ads.

Style: Brush, drawn letter, typeset

Colour		Size:	Any

Materials: Paper, card

Direction

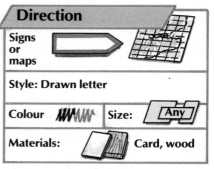

Signs or maps

Style: Drawn letter

Colour		Size:	Any

Materials: Card, wood

Identification

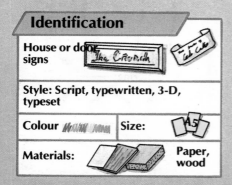

House or door signs

Style: Script, typewritten, 3-D, typeset

Colour		Size:	A5

Materials: Paper, wood

Warning

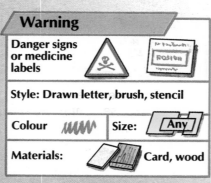

Danger signs or medicine labels

Style: Drawn letter, brush, stencil

Colour		Size:	Any

Materials: Card, wood

Announcement

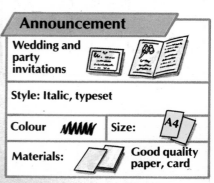

Wedding and party invitations

Style: Italic, typeset

Colour		Size:	A4

Materials: Good quality paper, card

Celebration

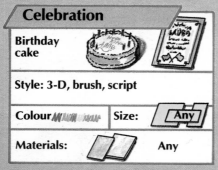

Birthday cake

Style: 3-D, brush, script

Colour		Size:	Any

Materials: Any

Presentation

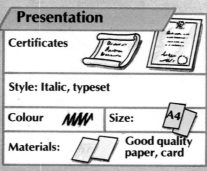

Certificates

Style: Italic, typeset

Colour		Size:	A4

Materials: Good quality paper, card

Story

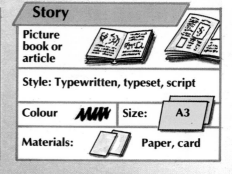

Picture book or article

Style: Typewritten, typeset, script

Colour		Size:	A3

Materials: Paper, card

Printing methods

In case you want to reproduce your work, various printing methods are explained below.

Photocopying D.I.Y.

Up to 50 copies

Access. Libraries and instant print shops.

Reasonable quality text. Some pictures may suffer.

Colour available, but expensive.

Up to A3 size

Stencil duplicating D.I.Y.

A stencil duplicator forces ink through a stencil onto paper.

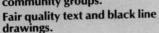

Up to 3,000 copies

Access. Schools, instant print shops, community groups.

Fair quality text and black line drawings.

A4 size.

Screen printing D.I.Y.

Screen printing is a type of stencil printing, in which ink of any colour is forced through a screen onto paper with a rubber blade (called a "squeegee").

Very slow.

Excellent results with large solid areas of colour, but not small text.

Up to A2 size.

Can print on any flat surface (e.g. T-shirts, wood, plastic, card).

Access. Schools and community groups. Art shops sell cheap kits.

Commercial printing

There are many types of commercial printing available for professional quality work. Most towns have instant print shops.

Understand the problem

Whether designing a poster for a charity sale or a magazine, the first priority is to understand the message and its purpose.

Read the message (along with any brief you may have) and break it down into its main components.

Brief

Copy

Ring the components. Number the components according to their order of importance.

These components are of equal importance, so are given the same number.

Each component needs to be made to look separate and more or less important than the other parts.

Thumbnail sketches (see page 7) are a good way of trying out different ideas.

Making things stand out

There are lots of design elements you can use to make parts of a message stand out, shown below. But things usually stand out most when they are different.

Size:
The biggest burger in the world!

Boldness:
Learn to ride a **Wheeler** bike.

Italic:
Suddenly, Lizzie saw a *huge* spider.

Underscore:
Congratulations on your birthday.

Devices:
*Aunty Flo *Cousin Spike

Directional elements:
Now turn the page ➔

Colour:
The colour this year is red

Borders:
Bike for sale Very cheap

Capitals:
Take a trip to KENYA

Different style:
Live performance by Track

Slant:
Don't lose your way.

Isolation:
Phil Over   The star

Decorated or large initial:
Claude Back, the lion tamer

Reversed lettering:
Black and white

Coloured background:
Sponsored fun run

Condensed type:
It was a tight squeeze

Expanded type:
Everyone spread out

Distortion:
Spike blew a BUBBLE

Descriptive lettering:
CRASH

You can use one or a combination of these techniques to emphasize the most important parts of your message. But don't overdo things.

Paste-up

Paste-up is the process of assembling all the components of a design – *typesetting* or hand-lettering and any *pictures* – ready for printing.

This page shows how to do paste-up which includes line illustrations to be printed in black.

Line illustration   Tone illustration   Colour illustration

Grid drawn on thin card.

For paste-up you need a *grid* (see page 33) drawn in blue pencil.

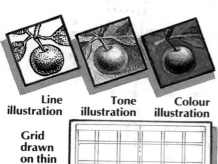

1

First take photocopies of all the components for the page or spread and cut them up.

2

Trace main outlines of grid.

Slip the grid under tracing paper and stick the copies in place to make sure everything fits. Remove the grid.

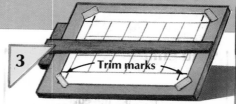

3

Trim marks

Use a ruler if you don't have a T-square.

If you have a drawing board, tape the grid to it and use a T-square to draw trim marks on it in black ink.

4

Carefully trim the originals to within about 3mm of the edge.

5

Apply glue to the back of each piece.

6

Make sure each piece is straight by using a T-square or ruler.

Carefully position each piece on the grid according to your rough paste-up.

7

Re-check for straightness by looking end-on across the page. Cover the paste-up with paper to protect it.

DESIGN TIPS — Optical illusions

In lettering you often need to distort apparently correct proportions to compensate for optical illusions.

*All curved and pointed parts of letters should extend beyond the guide lines.

These letters will look too small if drawn within the guide lines.

If you sit curved parts on the guidelines, the letters will look too small.

*In styles with thick and thin strokes, the widest part of curves is thicker than the thickest stem of a straight letter. This avoids it looking too thin.

*Diagonal strokes may need to be thinner towards the point at which they meet.

Diagonal strokes may need to be thinner than vertical strokes, or they can look too heavy.

*The stem strokes of capitals must be thicker than those of small letters.

*The centre bars of B, E, F and H need to be slightly above the true centre to avoid looking too low.

Copying alphabets

On the next four pages are alphabets to copy and use. You may also want to copy other alphabets. First trace the letters you want and then enlarge or reduce them.

Tracing

Trace the letters you want as shown below.

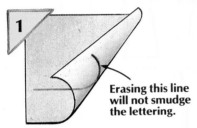

On the back of a piece of tracing paper, draw a guide line in pencil.

Trace the letters to make up the words you want.

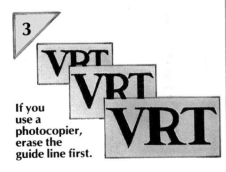

If you use a photocopier, erase the guide line first.

Enlarge or reduce the lettering to the size you want, either by the grid method (shown on the right) or by using a photocopier with enlarging/reducing facilities.

Grid enlarging

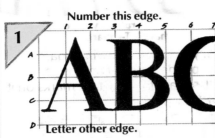

Number this edge.

Letter other edge.

Draw a grid over the lettering as shown.

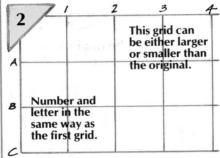

This grid can be either larger or smaller than the original.

Number and letter in the same way as the first grid.

Draw another grid the size you want the lettering to be.

Use the grid lines as a guide to drawing the letters freehand.

Paint or ink in the lettering as shown on page 18.

Making a lettering sheet

You may want to use letters of the same size for lots of different things. A lettering sheet is a quick way of doing this. The steps below show how to make one.

AAAAABBBCCCC
DDDDEEEEEEFFF
GGGHHHHIIIIIJJK
KLLLLMMM NNN
NNOOOOOPPPQ
QRRRRRSSSSSTT
TTTUUUUVVWW
WXX YYYZZ

Letters are repeated according to the frequency of their use in English.

Trace and enlarge the alphabet you want as shown below to make a master sheet.

Take photocopies of the master sheet.

Don't cut up the master sheet.

Cut up letters as needed and paste them together to compose words.

Either take a copy or trace off the lettering and ink or colour it as you want.

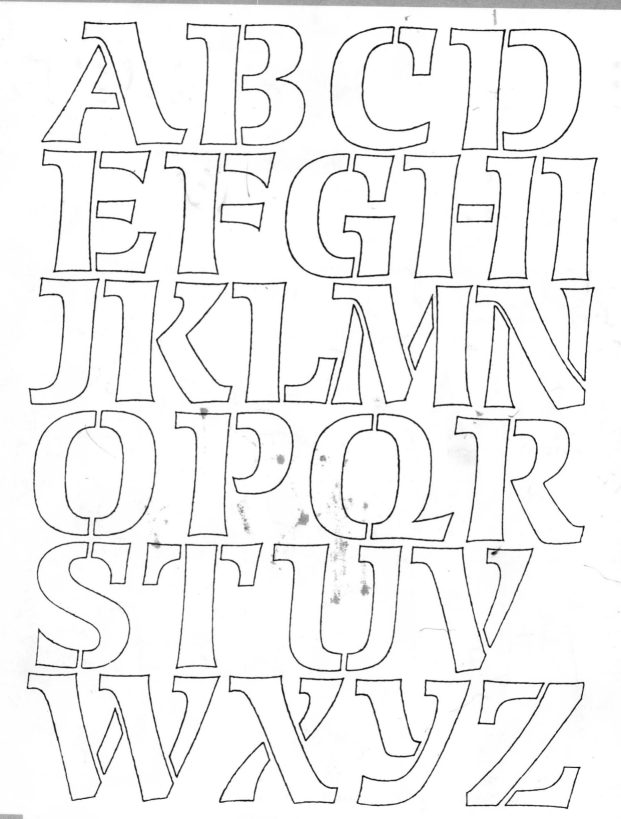

abcdefghijklmn
opqrstuvwxyz
ABCDEFGHIJ
KLMNOPQRS
TUVWXYZ
1234567890
?!&£$..::-'""

HUNTINGDON Designed by Jonathan Coleclough 1986

abcdefghijkl
mnopqrstuv
wxyzABCDE
FGHIJKLMN
OPQRSTUV
WXYZ12345
67890?!:"£&

CUMBRIA Designed by Wilf Dickie 1986

ABCDEFGH

IJKLMNOPQ

RSTUVWX

YZ&.,;;""""!?

-()-*/%$¢12

34567890

abcdefghijklm
nopqrstuvw
xyz ABCDEF
GHIJKLMNO
PQRSTUVW
XYZ 12345678
90:;,."?!$£"(%)

PALATINO Designed by Hermann Zapf 1950

abcdefghijkl
mnopqrstuv
wxyz ABCD
EFGHIJKLM
NOPQRSTU
VWXYZ
1234567890
;:,."?!$£"(%)

abcdefghijkl
mnopqrstuvw
xyz ABCDEFG
HIJKLMNOPQ
RSTUVWXYZ
1234567890
:;,."?!$£"(%)

FUTURA Designed by Paul Renner about 1928

Equipment and materials

Below is a list of the basic equipment and materials mentioned in this book. You can buy all these things from art shops and some stationers.

Media and materials

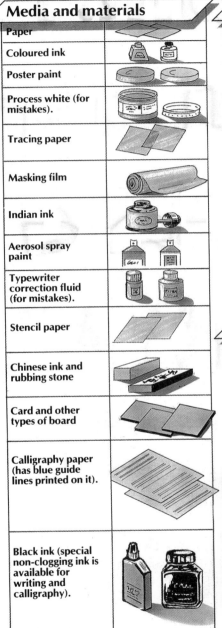

Paper	
Coloured ink	
Poster paint	
Process white (for mistakes).	
Tracing paper	
Masking film	
Indian ink	
Aerosol spray paint	
Typewriter correction fluid (for mistakes).	
Stencil paper	
Chinese ink and rubbing stone	
Card and other types of board	
Calligraphy paper (has blue guide lines printed on it).	
Black ink (special non-clogging ink is available for writing and calligraphy).	

Drawing equipment

Drawing board	
T-square	
Set square	
Ruler	
Rubber	
Scissors	
Depth scale	
Sticky tape	
French curve	
Flexible curve	
Pair of compasses	
Scalpel or craft knife	
Glue	

Paper sizes

The most commonly used paper sizes accord with the ISO (International Organization for Standardization) "A" series. This is based on a size called "AO", with an area of one square metre. Each size is half the next largest size up.

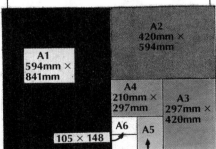

- A2 420mm × 594mm
- A1 594mm × 841mm
- A4 210mm × 297mm
- A3 297mm × 420mm
- A6 105 × 148
- A5 148mm × 210mm
- AO 841mm × 1189mm

Writing tools

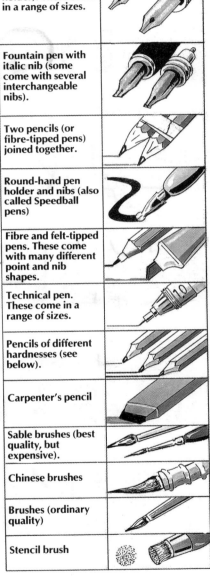

Witch pen (metal nib fixed to a holder). These come in a range of sizes.	
Fountain pen with italic nib (some come with several interchangeable nibs).	
Two pencils (or fibre-tipped pens) joined together.	
Round-hand pen holder and nibs (also called Speedball pens)	
Fibre and felt-tipped pens. These come with many different point and nib shapes.	
Technical pen. These come in a range of sizes.	
Pencils of different hardnesses (see below).	
Carpenter's pencil	
Sable brushes (best quality, but expensive).	
Chinese brushes	
Brushes (ordinary quality)	
Stencil brush	

Pencil hardnesses

7B Very soft	B	H	4H
6B	HB Medium	2H	5H
5B	F	3H	6H Very hard
4B			
3B			
2B			

Artwork. Lettering and/or pictures ready for reproduction.

Ascender. A stroke extending above the main part *(x height)* of a small letter.

Base line. The imaginary line on which letters and other characters appear to sit.

Bleed. Where an *illustration* or photograph extends beyond a cut edge of a page.

Box rule. A line drawn round *text* and/or pictures.

Bullet. Dots to highlight points in the *text*.

Calligraphy. Literally, "beautiful writing".

Caption. *Text* accompanying an *illustration* or photograph.

Cicero. A unit of measurement used in *typography* in Europe. 12 *Didot points* = 1 cicero.

Construction line. Lightly drawn pencil line.

Copy. The particular version of a *text* used for *typesetting*.

Copy fitting (or casting off). The preliminary measurement of *copy* to estimate the space it will occupy in a given size of type.

Depth scale. A special ruler marked in *point* sizes, used to measure the depth of a given number of lines of *typesetting*.

Descender. A stroke extending below the main part *(x height)* of a small letter.

Didot point. A unit of measurement used in *typography* in Europe. 1 Didot *point* = 0.376mm.

Em. The square of any given type size. The 12pt em *(pica* em) is used for linear measurements.

Folio. A page number.

Font/fount (or character set). A complete set of characters of a particular type size.

Graphic element. Any component part of a message, e.g. letter, *rule*, *illustration* and so on.

Grid. The framework of lines marking the margins and columns of a page and used as an aid in designing.

Gutter. The margins where two pages meet at a fold.

Heading (or headline). A title that draws attention to part of a *text*.

Illustration. A hand-produced picture.

Indent. A blank space at the beginning of a line, usually at the start of a paragraph or other item.

Justified. Lines of type of the same length, making straight-sided columns.

Label. A very short *caption*, often with an arrow.

Layout (page design). A plan showing the arrangement of words and pictures.

Line feed. The distance between lines of *text*, measured from *base line* to base line.

Margin. The outer blank areas surrounding the words and pictures.

Marking up. Writing instructions on *copy* for *typesetting*.

Orphan. A short line or single word at the foot of a page or column of *text*.

Paste-up. The process of assembling *text* and pictures ready for reproduction.

Pica. A unit of linear measurement used in *typography*. 12 *points* = 1 pica.

Point. The traditional unit of measurement in *typography*. 12 points = 1 pica (or *cicero*).

Rule. Horizontal and vertical lines, often used to divide up parts of the message.

Run-around. Type set to fit around the edge of a picture.

Sans serif (or sanserif). Type without *serifs*.

Serif. Strokes which finish off the ends of a letter's stems, arms and other parts.

Spread. Two pages side by side.

Subhead. A secondary level of *heading*.

Text. The words.

Tint. A coloured area, composed of minute dots or lines to produce a paler version of a solid colour.

Trim (or crop marks). Marks outside the page showing where the paper is to be cut.

Typeface. The name for a particular design of type.

Typesetting. The process of assembling type to form words.

Typography. The study and design of printed and other graphic messages.

Unjustified. *Text* setting in which the column of lines is straight on one side and irregular on the other.

Widow. A short line at the head of a page or column.

x height. The height of a small x.

Going further

Some useful books to read are suggested below.

Creative Lettering, Michael Harvey, The Bodley Head, 1985

Lettering Tips, Bill Gray, Van Nostrand Reinhold, 1983

Tips on Type, Bill Gray, Van Nostrand Reinhold, 1983

The Complete Guide to Calligraphy, Judy Martin, Phaidon, 1984

The Alternative Printing Handbook, Chris Treweek and Jonathan Zeitlyn, Penguin, 1983

Mastering Calligraphy, Tom Gourdie, Search Press, 1984

Lettering Techniques, John Lancaster, Batsford, 1982

Calligraphy Techniques, John Lancaster, Batsford, 1986

Layout and Design for Calligraphers, Alan Furber, Dryad Press, 1985

Typography, Ruari McLean, Thames and Hudson, 1980

Manual of Graphic Techniques 3, Tom Porter and Sue Goodman, Astragal Books, 1983

Answers to puzzle on page 4

1 Eras
2 Century Schoolbook
3 Gill Sans
4 Melior

PART TWO
TECHNICAL DRAWING

Susan Peach

Edited by Tony Potter

Consultant editor : Colin Rattray

(Lecturer at Middlesex Polytechnic
and freelance technical artist)

Technical consultant : Colin Motteram

Designed by Iain Ashman

Illustrated by Chris Lyon

Additional illustrations by
Guy Smith, Peter Bull,
Mick Posen, Martin Newton,
Steve Cross and Jeremy Gower.

Contents

About this section

This section is a guide to technical drawing and illustration for beginners.

It shows the stages involved in designing and drawing objects, starting with rough sketches and models. You can also find out about special methods of drawing, called orthographic and isometric projections and perspective.

To start with, you do not need any special equipment – just a ruler and pencils. A smooth table top will do as a drawing board.

At the back of the section you can find out about more complicated drawing equipment, and about common abbreviations and symbols used to simplify drawings.

You can also find out how to colour and mount your drawings for displays and exhibitions, and how to use photographs.

Glossary

Technical drawing is full of unusual words. These are explained in the glossary on page 95, and are highlighted in the section each time you come across them, like this: *isometric*.

What is technical drawing?

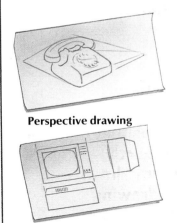

Perspective drawing

Orthographic projection

Technical drawing is a means of communicating instructions and information to people to help them make or build things, or imagine how they will look when made.

Some sorts of technical drawings, such as *perspective drawings*, give general information about what an object actually looks like.

Other drawings, like *orthographic projections*, give precise information about the size and shape of an object, so that someone could make it from the instructions on the drawing.

In technical drawing a series of rules, called *conventions*, are used to simplify the drawings and to ensure that they are easily understood. This means that a drawing can be passed from one person to another, or even sent to another country where a different language is used, and still be understood.

Who uses technical drawings?

Technical drawings are widely used in all the professions which involve designing, building or making objects. They are used to pass detailed technical information about the size, shape and construction of an object from the designer to the person who will make the object.

Architects and civil engineers use technical drawings to show builders how to construct a building and what materials to use.

Mechanical engineers use technical drawings to pass instructions to the factory about how to make their designs.

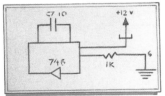

Electronic engineers do technical drawings to design circuits and show how they are wired up.

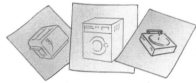

Product designers produce technical drawings to show clients what their ideas will look like when the product is made.

Getting started

You do not have to spend a lot of money on technical drawing equipment, as the basic tools and equipment, shown below, are simple and cheap. All you need is a flat surface to work on (a desk or table), a plastic ruler, compasses, 60°/30° and 45° set squares, a protractor, some sharp pencils, masking tape and paper.

If you want to invest in some more specialized equipment, there are suggestions below for professional tools to buy and how to use them.

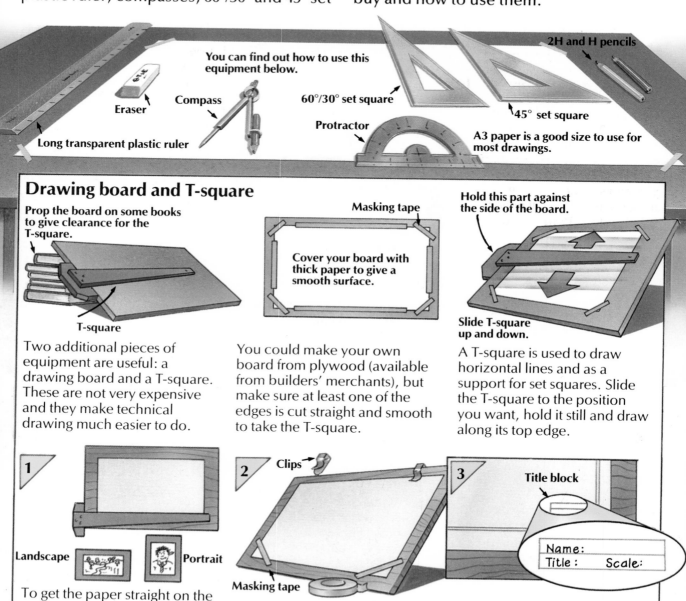

You can find out how to use this equipment below.

Eraser

Compass

60°/30° set square

45° set square

2H and H pencils

Protractor

Long transparent plastic ruler

A3 paper is a good size to use for most drawings.

Drawing board and T-square

Prop the board on some books to give clearance for the T-square.

T-square

Masking tape

Cover your board with thick paper to give a smooth surface.

Hold this part against the side of the board.

Slide T-square up and down.

Two additional pieces of equipment are useful: a drawing board and a T-square. These are not very expensive and they make technical drawing much easier to do.

You could make your own board from plywood (available from builders' merchants), but make sure at least one of the edges is cut straight and smooth to take the T-square.

A T-square is used to draw horizontal lines and as a support for set squares. Slide the T-square to the position you want, hold it still and draw along its top edge.

1

Landscape   Portrait

To get the paper straight on the board, move the T-square to the bottom of the board and line the paper up against it. There are two ways of positioning paper, shown above.

2 Clips

Masking tape

The paper has to be attached to the board so that it does not move around while you are drawing. You can do this with masking tape, sticky tape or drawing board clips.

3 Title block

Name:
Title :   Scale:

Your drawing will look neater if you pencil in a border line 10mm from the edge, and a title block to show your name, the title and scale of the drawing.

Paper

Various types of paper are used for technical drawing. Layout or cartridge paper is used for pencil drawings and plans. Tracing paper is used with marker pens and for tracing over photos. You can find out about different sizes of paper on page 86.

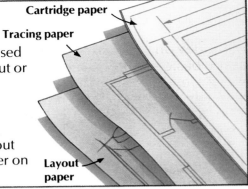

Cartridge paper

Tracing paper

Layout paper

Pencils and pens

Pencils come in different hardnesses*, H or 2H pencils are best for drawing with instruments, while softer HB or 2B pencils are good for drawing freehand. Pencils must be kept sharp to draw fine and accurate lines.

A pencil sharpener gives a sharp round point.

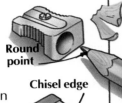

Round point

You can also rub the lead on glass paper to get a chisel edge, which draws a very fine line.

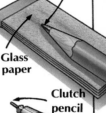

Chisel edge

Glass paper

Clutch pencils are useful, as they do not need to be sharpened.

Clutch pencil

To do ink line drawings you need a technical pen with a point thickness of about 0.2mm.

Technical pen

Set squares and protractor

Set squares are used to draw lines at 90°, 60°, 45° and 30°, angles which are frequently needed. Set squares are made of transparent plastic so that you can see the drawing underneath. You will need two: a 45° and a 60°/30° set square.

Lines at 90°

Lines at 45°

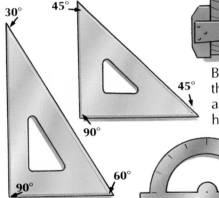

30°   45°

45°

90°

90°   60°

By holding a set square against the T-square you can draw lines at 90°, 45°, 60° and 30° to the horizontal.

You also need a protractor to measure other angles.

Compasses

Compasses are used to draw *arcs* and circles. You can use an ordinary compass, but a spring bow compass, shown on the right, is best as it can not slip out of position.

To avoid the compass point slipping or making holes in the paper, stick a piece of masking tape over the centre of the circle to be drawn. This will hold the point in position.

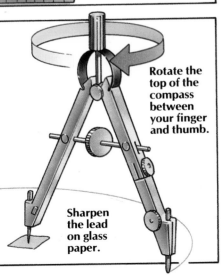

Rotate the top of the compass between your finger and thumb.

Sharpen the lead on glass paper.

Other useful things

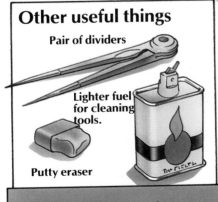

Pair of dividers

Lighter fuel for cleaning tools.

Putty eraser

You will find information about more complicated drawing equipment on page 86-87.

Stages in design

To get from an initial idea to a finished product, there are several design stages. This is often called the *design process*. As part of this process, a designer uses technical drawings to illustrate and explain ideas.

These pages show a flow chart of the nine main stages involved. A designer does not have to go through all the stages, or always in the same order.

You could try designing something at home to see how the design process works. As an example there are some tips on these pages for designing a cassette rack, but you can use the same stages for anything you design.

Flow chart

The chart below is a summary of the main stages in the design process. Follow the arrows below and on these pages to see different routes you can take.

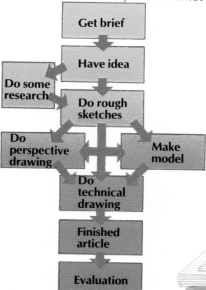

- Get brief
- Have idea
- Do some research
- Do rough sketches
- Do perspective drawing
- Make model
- Do technical drawing
- Finished article
- Evaluation

The brief

First, someone (called the client) asks a designer to design something. The client gives the designer a brief – a set of instructions about what the design will be used for, what it must look like and how much it can cost.

A written brief →

Design a cassette rack
To store about 10 cassettes
Made of wood or plastic
To fit on a shelf

The idea

Designers come up with ideas for the design which follow the brief. They think about what the object will be used for and what it could look like.

You could get ideas for your design from shops or pictures in magazines.

Research

The designer has to know how the object being designed is to be made, as this helps work out the details. Designers often consult with engineers and other experts, or do research to discover what they need to know.

At home, this could mean borrowing books from the library and reading up on the subject.

Sketches

Ideas are often developed as small rough sketches (called *thumbnails*). Lots of ideas can be quickly tried out until one is found that works.

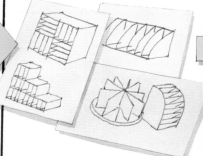

You will find that doing pencil sketches of the cassette rack helps you work out your ideas.

Find out more about sketching on pages 56-57.

Perspective drawing

Designers often do a realistic three-dimensional picture of their design, called a *perspective* drawing. This is cheaper and quicker than making a model, but still shows the client how the product will look.

You may find a perspective drawing useful to show other people what your rack looks like.

Find out how to do perspective drawings on pages 72-75.

Model

Making a model is an easy way of testing that a design works. Designers often make models (called *mock-ups*) to show clients how the finished product will look.

To try out your rack you could make a mock-up from card. This helps check that the parts fit together.

Your model can be full-size or to scale.

You can find how to make card models like this on pages 58-61.

Technical drawing

Technical drawings convey precise information about an object's size and shape to the person who will make it. The plans that the designer has drawn up are passed on to someone else (like a builder, carpenter or engineer) to show them how to make the design.

At home, technical drawings are the most accurate way of working out the details of something you want to make, such as its shape and sizes, called *dimensions*.

Orthographic projection

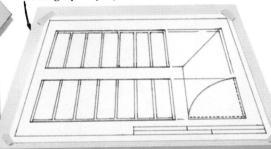

Orthographic projections show the different sides of an object, all drawn facing the viewer. They also give exact information about its size and how the parts fit together.

You can find out how to do orthographic projections on pages 62-67.

Isometric projection

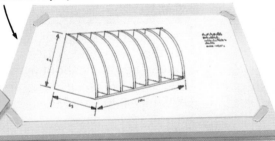

Isometric projections are three-dimensional, and are used to give accurate scale measurements of an object.

You can find out how to do isometric projections on pages 70-71.

The finished article and evaluation

Next the article is made. The final stage of the design process is called evaluation. This is when the designer assesses how successful the design has been – if it has fulfilled the brief and if it could be improved.

Sketching

When you have an idea for something to design, the first stage is often to do some quick freehand sketches of what you want it to look like. Professional designers often do lots of tiny sketches, called *thumbnails*, to try out their ideas.

On these pages you can find out how a sketch can be useful, whatever you are designing, and read some tips on making sketching easier.

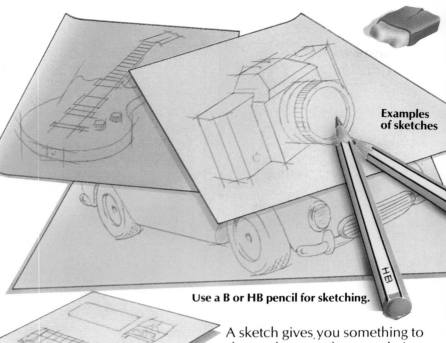

Examples of sketches

Use a B or HB pencil for sketching.

Why do a sketch?

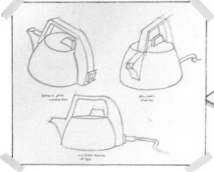

A sketch gives you something to show other people to get their advice on your ideas.

Sketching helps to sort out your ideas – you can quickly try out different designs to see which looks best.

A sketch is good preparation for more complicated technical drawings. It helps work out the *layout** on the page.

Sketching tips

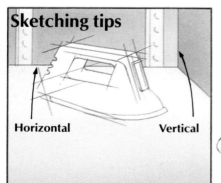

Horizontal   **Vertical**

Start your drawing with any vertical and horizontal lines in the surroundings, as these act as reference points for the rest of the drawing.

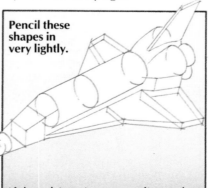

Pencil these shapes in very lightly.

If the object is a complicated shape, try drawing it as a series of boxes and cylinders. Sketch these shapes in first as a framework for the outline.

This is called negative space.

Remember to look at the space around the object as well. Think about the object's position in relation to its surroundings.

*The layout is the arrangement of a drawing on the paper.

Sketching from start to finish

When you design something you often need to sketch it from your imagination. Drawing real objects is good practice for this.

Here you can find out how to go about doing a sketch, from start to finish. A telephone is used as an example, but you could sketch any object.

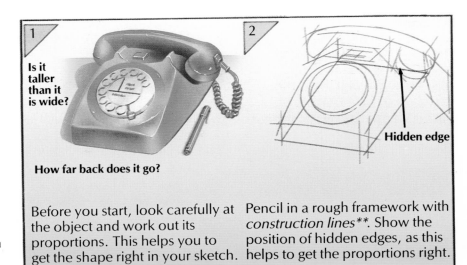

1 Is it taller than it is wide?

How far back does it go?

2 Hidden edge

Before you start, look carefully at the object and work out its proportions. This helps you to get the shape right in your sketch.

Pencil in a rough framework with *construction lines**. Show the position of hidden edges, as this helps to get the proportions right.

3 This angle shows how long the receiver is.

Imagine lines at angles between various parts of the object to help you check the size and proportion of the parts in relation to one another.

4 Erase the construction lines.

For a rough sketch you may not need to draw more than the main outline. If you want to add details, such as the dial holes, do this last.

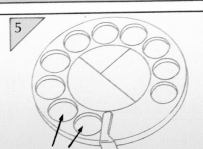

5 These holes are actually round, but look oval.

Look at the object repeatedly while you are drawing to check what you see. Always draw what you see, not what you know the object looks like.

Getting the proportions right

If you work on a drawing for a long time you may not notice any errors building up, so it is best to check the shape and proportions regularly.

Try squinting at your drawing or looking at it in the mirror to get a new view.

Try not to press too hard with the pencil until you are happy with the proportions.

A good way to judge proportions is to measure your object with a pencil, as shown on the right.

1 Hold a pencil out at arm's length and shut one eye.

2 Line up the pencil with a short upright or horizontal edge on the subject.

3 "Mark" the length on the pencil with your thumb.

4 Keep your thumb still, and count how many times this length fits into other lengths on the object.

5 Check that the proportions are the same on your sketch.

**These are faint lines used to construct the rough shape before you draw the outline.*

Models

Designers often produce models, called *mock-ups*, to check that their design works and to show their clients. On these pages you can find out how to make a cube from paper or thin card, and how to adapt it to make other exciting models, like a house and a truck. The models are made from *developments*, which are plans showing all the sides of an object opened out on to one *plane* (surface).

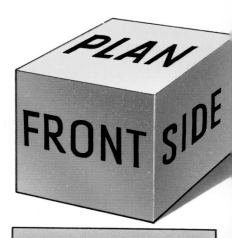

Making a cube

Things you will need:

Strong glue

Sharp craft knife or scalpel

Piece of A4 card or paper

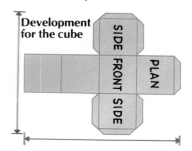

Development for the cube

SIDE
FRONT
PLAN
SIDE
FRONT
SIDE

Keep the cube – you will be able to use it on page 63.

1

20mm

75mm

Fix the card to your drawing board with masking tape. Make sure that the card is square to the board. With a 2H pencil, draw a horizontal line 75mm up from the bottom of the card, and a vertical one 20mm from the left-hand side.

2

Measure each square from line A to stop errors building up.

Line A

60mm   120mm   180mm

Where the lines cross, measure 60mm to the right and 60mm up. Using a T-square and set square, complete the square. Add on the remaining five squares, as shown on the development.

3

PLAN

Centre lines to position lettering.

Draw in 8mm-wide tabs for sticking the cube together as shown on the development. (Note: if you want to use the cube on page 63, write "Front", "Side" and "Plan" on the faces shown.)

4

Use the ruler as a guide.

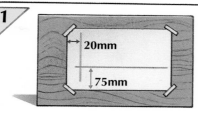

Place the ruler along the line to be cut and hold down firmly.

Cut the shape out, using a craft knife or a scalpel. Score along all the lines to be bent by running the knife over them once only.

5

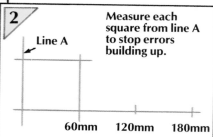

Fold up like this.

Colour in the cube. You could use marker pens – there are some tips on how to use them on page 77. Then fold the cube along the scored lines and glue it together.

A gift box

The cube can easily be adapted to make a gift box. The arrangement of the tabs on the development above is slightly different, as you will need tabs on the lid to hold the box closed, as shown below.

Development for the gift box

Making a truck

The developments for the truck below are on page 93. Enlarge* them on to cartridge paper, paint or colour them, then cut out the pieces.

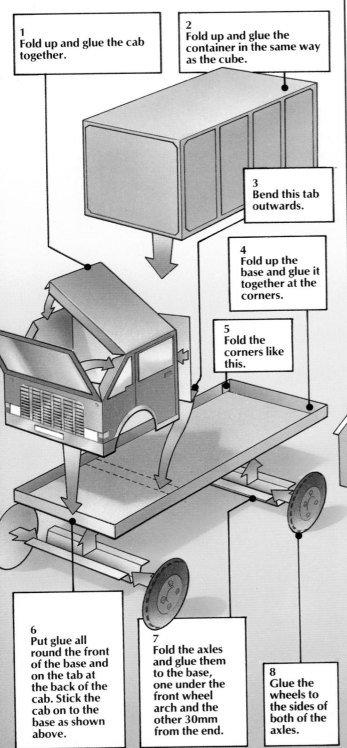

1 Fold up and glue the cab together.

2 Fold up and glue the container in the same way as the cube.

3 Bend this tab outwards.

4 Fold up the base and glue it together at the corners.

5 Fold the corners like this.

6 Put glue all round the front of the base and on the tab at the back of the cab. Stick the cab on to the base as shown above.

7 Fold the axles and glue them to the base, one under the front wheel arch and the other 30mm from the end.

8 Glue the wheels to the sides of both of the axles.

Making a house

1 Copy the developments from page 92 and enlarge* them on to cartridge paper. If you want to colour the model, do it while it is flat. Then cut out the pieces with a sharp knife.

2

Glue here.

Bend back the tabs at the bottom of the house and porch walls and glue them to the inside to reinforce the base.

3 Fold the walls and glue them together. Fold the roof and glue it to the walls. You could leave the model like this and make it a cottage.

Glue here.

These tabs overhang on the outside.

4

Stick on here.

Fold up the porch walls and glue the tabs on to the front wall. Fold up the porch roof and glue it on to the porch walls and the roof.

5 Cut out the balcony arches, leaving the flap at the bottom as a support. Fold and glue the tabs to the main building.

Glue on here.

6

Fold up the chimney and glue it together. Glue the chimney to the porch roof.

*You can find out how to enlarge the plans on page 94.

59

Modelling tips

Models can be made from a variety of different materials. The models shown here are made from cheap and simple things that you may have at home.

On these pages you can find out about some of the techniques used for working with card, Plasticine and polystyrene. These tips will help you to make simple models of your own designs.

Successful model-making depends on accurate measurements and cutting, so it is best to work out things like the scale and the shape of parts first.

Construction kits

Construction kits are useful for making quick and simple models of your designs, and do not require any special techniques or artistic ability to make effective, good-looking models.

Special components like doors, windows and wheels make models of buildings and vehicles even easier to do. You can also use these parts for the other models described on these pages.

Plasticine

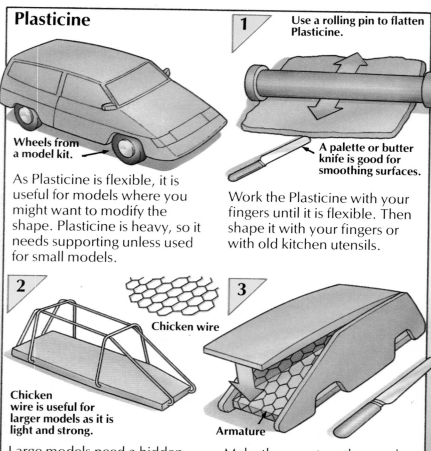

Wheels from a model kit.

As Plasticine is flexible, it is useful for models where you might want to modify the shape. Plasticine is heavy, so it needs supporting unless used for small models.

1 Use a rolling pin to flatten Plasticine.

A palette or butter knife is good for smoothing surfaces.

Work the Plasticine with your fingers until it is flexible. Then shape it with your fingers or with old kitchen utensils.

2 Chicken wire is useful for larger models as it is light and strong.

Large models need a hidden skeleton, called an armature, to support them. Armatures can be made from things like wood, wire or cardboard.

Chicken wire

3 Armature

Make the armature the rough size and shape of the model, cover it with Plasticine and then mould the material to the final shape.

Polystyrene

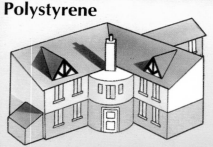

Expanded polystyrene is good for making simple models that can be carved from a block. You can use blocks of polystyrene packing material.

1

Polystyrene can be easily cut with wood-working tools like saws and rasps. Smaller details can be cut with a scalpel or craft knife.

Card

You can make complicated models like this spaceship by glueing a series of card *developments* together. It is best to sketch out the development first, to work out where to join the sides together and put tabs.

Make this part from an ice lolly stick.

1

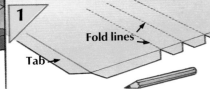

Fold lines

Tab

Draw the development on the card. To glue the model together there must be a tab on one side of any two edges to be joined.

2

Score folds on the outside of the model.

Before you glue your model together, score all fold lines with the back of the blade of a craft knife, using a ruler as a straight edge.

3

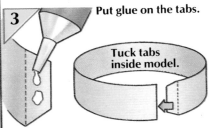

Put glue on the tabs.

Tuck tabs inside model.

Paper clips are useful for holding the pieces in place while the glue dries. When it has set, use a knife to remove any blobs of glue on the outside of the model.

4

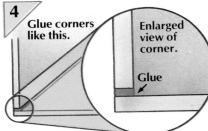

Glue corners like this.

Enlarged view of corner.

Glue

If you are using thick card which will not fold easily, it is better to cut the sides out separately and then stick them together as shown above.

5

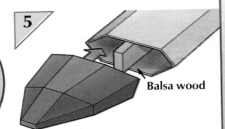

Balsa wood

Larger card and paper models may need a support to keep them rigid. A good support can be made from thin strips of balsa wood glued inside the card model.

2

You can use a wire brush to make any curved shapes. Use the brush to work away the surface of the block and create a curve.

3

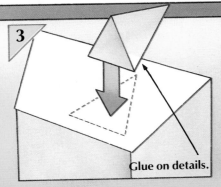

Glue on details.

To glue several pieces of polystyrene together, you must use a non-solvent glue* as other glues dissolve the surface of polystyrene.

4

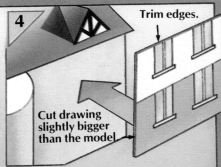

Trim edges.

Cut drawing slightly bigger than the model.

A good way to finish polystyrene models is to do a suitable drawing on paper, then glue it to the surface of the model.

Such as Copydex or a polystyrene cement.

Orthographic projection

Orthographic projection is a method of drawing an object by producing a series of flat views of its different sides. This means that all the object's features can be shown. Each side is seen in its true shape, unlike *perspective drawings*, which distort the view. Orthographic projections are used by engineers and architects to show detailed instructions about an object, so that it can be reproduced exactly.

There are six possible views of any object (see below), but three are usually enough to show all the features. These three views are called the *front*, *side* and *plan* views. The front and side can also be called the front and side *elevations*.

The views are positioned on the page in a fixed *layout*. There are two kinds of layout, called *first angle* and *third angle.* You can read about first angle below, and third angle on page 66-67.

Engineers and architects agree to draw things in either first or third angle in order to avoid any confusion when drawings are passed from one person to another – from the designer to the engineer, for example. All orthographic projections are marked to tell the viewer which layout has been used. The symbols used are:

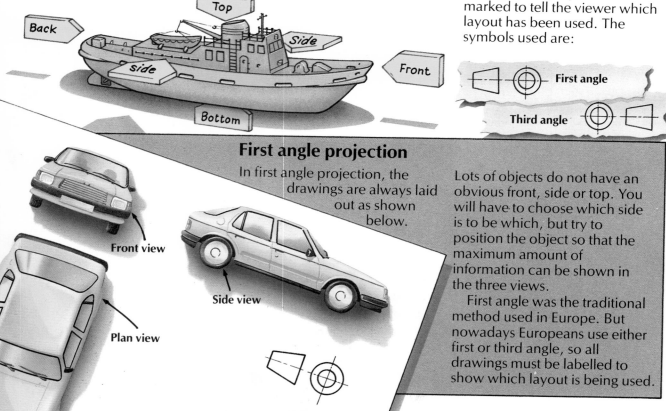

First angle projection

In first angle projection, the drawings are always laid out as shown below.

Lots of objects do not have an obvious front, side or top. You will have to choose which side is to be which, but try to position the object so that the maximum amount of information can be shown in the three views.

First angle was the traditional method used in Europe. But nowadays Europeans use either first or third angle, so all drawings must be labelled to show which layout is being used.

First angle drawings

Follow the steps below to find out why the views are laid out as they are for first angle projection. You will need:

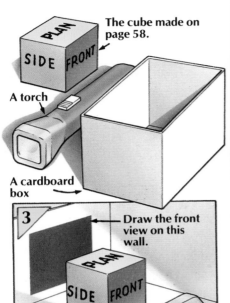

The cube made on page 58.

A torch

A cardboard box

1

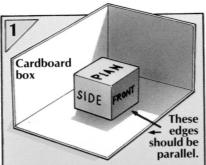

Cardboard box

These edges should be parallel.

Cut up a cardboard box to leave two sides and the base. Stand the cube inside the box with the plan face on top and the front and side faces towards you.

2

This is called the plan view.

Hold the cube in the air and shine a torch on the top face so that its shadow falls on the base of the box. This is where the view of the top face will be. Put the cube back on the base of the box and draw round it.

3

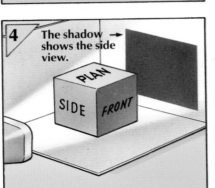

Draw the front view on this wall.

Shine the torch on to the front face of the cube so that the shadow is projected on to the box wall behind. The shadow shows the front view position.

4

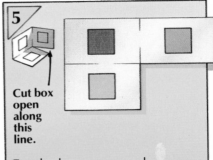

The shadow shows the side view.

Shine the torch on to the side face, so that its shadow is projected behind. Draw round the cube again. This is called the side or end view.

5

Cut box open along this line.

Cut the box open as shown and flatten it out. You can now see how the views are arranged on paper. They are always set out in the same pattern, so they do not need labels.

6

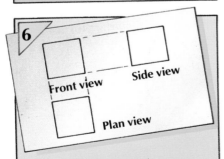

Front view   Side view

Plan view

The separate views are always shown in line with each other. Spaces are left between them for *dimensions* (length, breadth and other measurements) and other notes.

Drawing other objects

As all the cube's sides are the same shape, all the views are the same. Try sketching another object with sides of different shapes, using the steps shown above.

On your drawing the left side will be shown to the right of the front view.

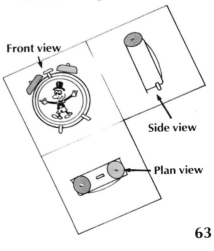

Front view

Side view

Plan view

First angle orthographic projection

Follow the steps shown on these pages to draw a *first angle* orthographic projection of any object. A cassette box is shown as an example, but the same method is used to do accurate drawings of anything, either a real object or something you are designing from your own imagination.

1 Before you start

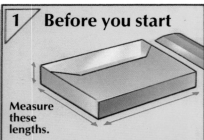

Measure these lengths.

First measure the object's length, width and height, as well as any other *dimensions* that will be needed. Note them on a piece of scrap paper.

2

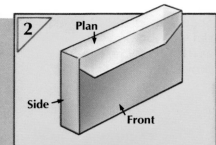

Plan

Side

Front

Decide which side is to be the *front*, which the *side* and which the *plan* view. It does not really matter which is which, as long as all the features are shown.

3

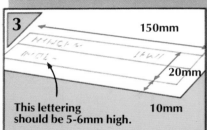

150mm

20mm

This lettering should be 5-6mm high.

10mm

Draw in a pencil border 10mm from the edges of the paper and a title block* in the bottom right-hand corner. The title block should show the title and *scale* of the drawing, your name and the date.

4

Always state which units you are using.

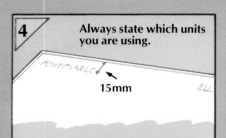

15mm

You must state that you are using first angle projection and that the dimensions are in millimetres. Write this on a line at the top of the paper or in the title block.

5

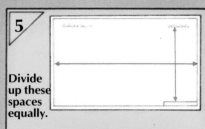

Divide up these spaces equally.

Work out the position of the views on the page. They need to be evenly spaced, not squashed up on one side. It is a good idea to do a sketch first to work out the rough *layout*.

Drawing to scale

It is not always possible to do full-size orthographic projections. Sometimes you will have to draw an object to scale – either larger or smaller than real life.

The scale is usually written as a *ratio* (a mathematical way of showing the proportion of one quantity to another). For example, if the drawing is half the size of the real object, the scale is written 1:2 – every one unit in the drawing represents two units in real life. If the drawing is five times as big as the object, the scale is 5:1.

You must tell the viewer the scale by showing the ratio in the title block.

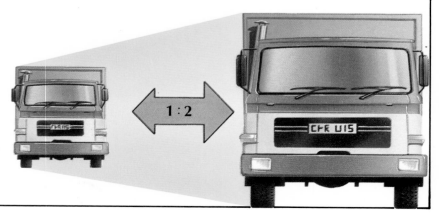

1 : 2

Doing the drawing

Lines

Different parts of the drawing are done in different lines*. The main ones are:

Construction lines – faint continuous lines used to plot out the basic shapes and for *projection* and *dimension lines* (see below). Use a 4H pencil.

Outlines – firm continuous lines used to show the outline of the object. Outlines are often drawn over construction lines. Use a 2H pencil.

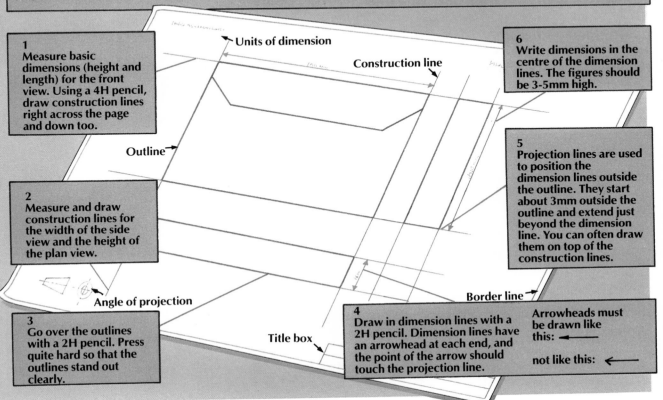

Units of dimension

Construction line

Outline

Angle of projection

Title box

Border line

1
Measure basic dimensions (height and length) for the front view. Using a 4H pencil, draw construction lines right across the page and down too.

2
Measure and draw construction lines for the width of the side view and the height of the plan view.

3
Go over the outlines with a 2H pencil. Press quite hard so that the outlines stand out clearly.

4
Draw in dimension lines with a 2H pencil. Dimension lines have an arrowhead at each end, and the point of the arrow should touch the projection line.

5
Projection lines are used to position the dimension lines outside the outline. They start about 3mm outside the outline and extend just beyond the dimension line. You can often draw them on top of the construction lines.

6
Write dimensions in the centre of the dimension lines. The figures should be 3-5mm high.

Arrowheads must be drawn like this: ◄—

not like this: ⟵

Lettering

Lettering in the title block and elsewhere on the drawing is normally done in capital letters. Small letters are only used in abbreviations**, and are done in printed writing.

Rub-down lettering looks neat. Rub each letter with the blunt end of a pencil to transfer it to your paper.

Rounded letters like o, b and p are larger than other letters, and need to sit just below the guideline to look even with other letters.

Spaces between letters should look the same size, even though they actually vary.

Letters should be the same height: about 5-6mm.

FULL SIZE

Pencil in guide lines to keep the letters neat.

1st tool box

These letters should sit below the line.

Remove mistakes by sticking a piece of masking tape over the letter, then peeling the tape and the letter off gently.

*There is more information on the lines used in technical drawing on page 90.

**There is a list of common abbreviations on page 90.

Third angle orthographic projection

These pages explain *third angle projection*, which is the most commonly used *layout*. Third angle is an alternative method of viewing an object to *first angle*.

Originally third angle was used in North America, but nowadays it is used in Europe too. First and third angle projections are equally acceptable and approved internationally.

Origin of first and third angle

In geometry, each of the four *quadrants* formed by the intersecting *planes* in the diagram is called one "angle". Those numbered 1 and 3 are used in *orthographic projection*.

Imagine that the object to be drawn is suspended in either the first or third angle. The *front* and *plan* views are projected on to the planes, which are then opened out in the direction of the arrows to give the layouts for first and third angle.

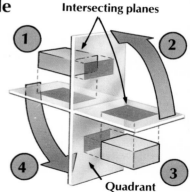

Intersecting planes

Quadrant

The use of the first and third angles rather than the second or fourth is just a *convention*.

1 Third angle views

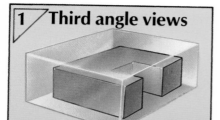

You can see how a third angle projection is laid out by imagining that the object to be drawn is suspended in the middle of a glass box.

2

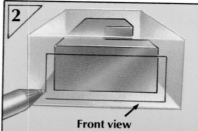

Front view

If you looked through each side of the box in turn you could draw on the glass the front, *side* and plan views of the object inside.

3

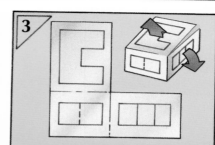

If the glass box were cut open and flattened out, you would end up with three views arranged as above. This is third angle layout.

Symbols

The symbols used to show which layout is being used are themselves orthographic projections. The symbols show the front and side views of a cone with the end cut off. In each case the side view shows the left-hand or narrower end of the object.

The first angle symbol shows the side view projected to the right of the front view.

First angle

The third angle symbol shows it in its true position : to the left of the front view.

Third angle

Advantages of third angle

In third angle the side and plan views are drawn in the same relationship to the front view as they are in real life : the plan is drawn above, and the side view is drawn at the side it represents. This makes third angle layout easier to understand, which is why it is becoming more widely used than first angle.

This side view shows the left-hand side of the object. It is drawn to the left of the front view.

The plan view, which shows the top of the object, is drawn above the front view.

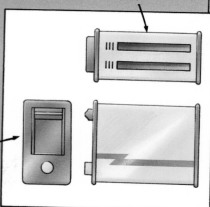

Third angle drawings

Apart from the layout, third angle drawings are done in the same way as first angle, with construction lines, outlines and so on. The tips below show you how to draw things like circular parts and hidden details.

Thin dashed lines like this are used to draw any hidden details which need to be shown, like the position of the batteries.

This side view shows the right-hand side of the radio, and in third angle is drawn to the right of the front view.

Dimensions of circular parts are shown like this. Do not use the *centre lines* as *dimension lines*. On the drawing, diameter is often abbreviated to ø.

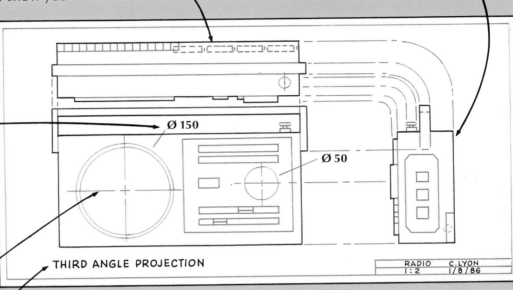

Ø 150

Ø 50

THIRD ANGLE PROJECTION

RADIO	C. LYON
1:2	1/8/86

Find the centre of circular parts by drawing two centre lines (thin *chain lines* with alternate long and short dashes) crossing at 90° where the centre is to be. Centre lines should not cross in the spaces between dashes, and they should extend outside the outline of the circle.

Do not forget to show which layout you are using.

Things to draw

You could practise drawing orthographic projections with other objects like these.

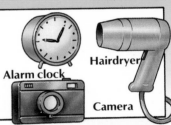

Alarm clock

Hairdryer

Camera

Orthographic projection puzzles

Here are some unusual views of household objects. See if you can work out what the objects are and which orthographic view is shown.*

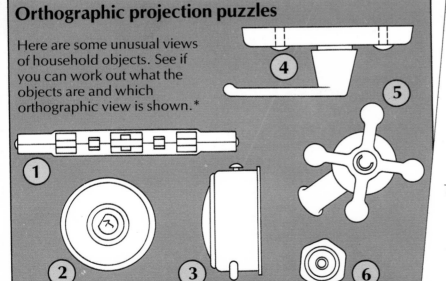

How to remember…

Try to remember this rhyme to remind you which layout is first angle and which is third angle.

For **a**ll **p**erfect **b**read,
Think and **p**lan **a**head.

The initial letters stand for:

First angle – **p**lan **b**elow,
Third angle – **p**lan **a**bove.

Architectural drawing

Orthographic *plan views* are often used by builders and architects to show the *layout* of buildings. They have special symbols to show common features like doors, windows and stairs. On these pages you can find out how to draw simple architectural plans using these symbols. Once you have mastered the basic *conventions*, you can use them to design your own exciting buildings.

Architectural conventions

This is an architectural plan of the ground floor of the house shown above. It is the kind of plan that builders use to lay out the foundations. On the plan you can see some of the common architectural features, and how to represent them.

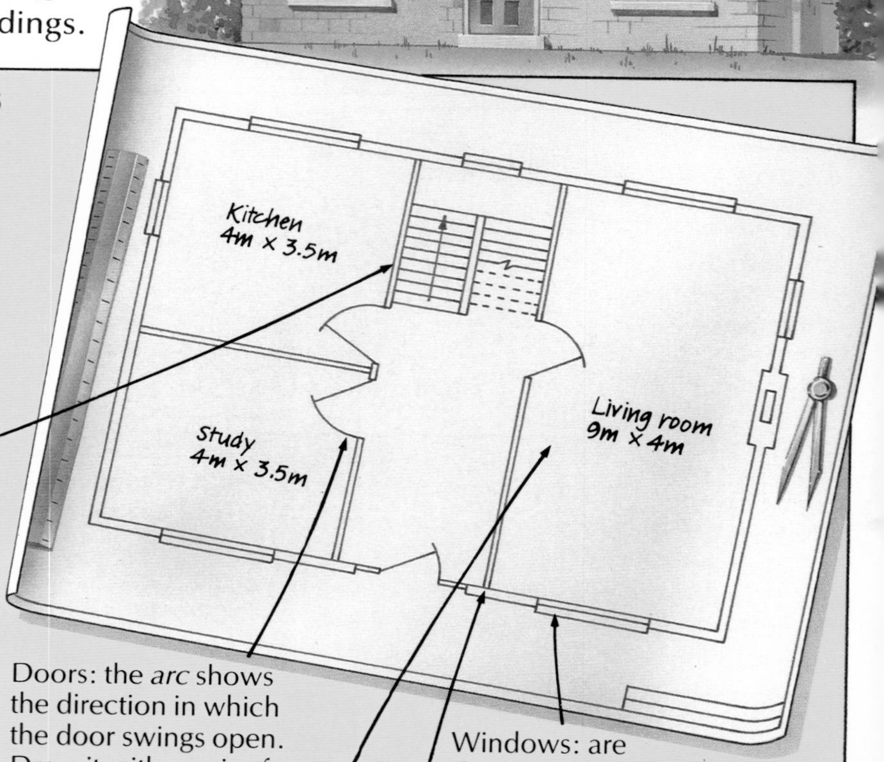

Stairs: The length of the staircase should be divided up equally into the number of stairs, as shown below. The stairs are numbered from the bottom and arrows are drawn to show the "up" direction.

Kitchen
4m × 3.5m

Study
4m × 3.5m

Living room
9m × 4m

How to space stairs

Top of stairs

Bottom of stairs

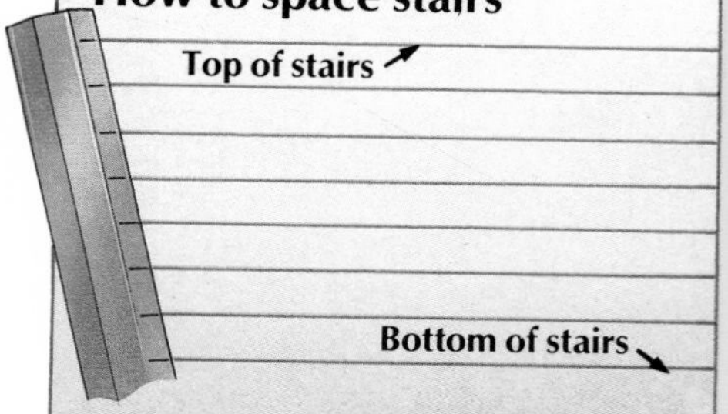

Here is how to divide up the space occupied by a staircase into (for example) seven stairs. Angle a ruler with the 0 at the top of the stairs and 70mm on the bottom, as shown above. Mark off every 10mm between the top and bottom. Draw parallel lines through the marks to divide up the space into seven stairs.

Doors: the *arc* shows the direction in which the door swings open. Draw it with a pair of compasses.

Dimensions: the room *dimensions* show the internal measurements from wall to wall, but do not include the thickness of the walls.

Walls: there are two main types of walls – outer walls and internal partitions. Partitions are usually built about 110mm thick, while outer walls are much thicker (about 300mm).

Windows: are drawn like this.

Scale: Architectural plans are always drawn to *scale*, which must be shown clearly on the drawing. A scale of 1:100 is easy to use, as each centimetre on the drawing will represent a metre in real life. You can find out more about scale on page 64.

To practise drawing house plans, you could copy this plan using your drawing equipment.

1 Draw your home

Before you start, measure the lengths of the walls in all the rooms to be shown. To do this you need a long tape measure, such as a dressmaker's or carpenter's tape.

2

Note the position and width of windows and doors, and which way the doors open. If your home is on more than one floor, remember to show the stairs.

3

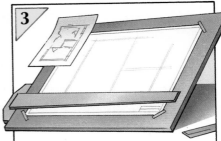

Next do a rough sketch to help you work out a suitable scale and page layout. Then you can do the final drawing with your equipment. Remember to show the scale.

Design your own buildings

You could try drawing plans of imaginary buildings, such as your ideal house, a farm, a fairy tale castle or a space station.

Here are the conventional ways of drawing some other features which you might like to include on your plans.

Sink
Cooker
Bath
W.C.
Basin
Spiral staircase

Try drawing front and side views to go with your plans. In architecture these are called *elevations.* Normally all four elevations are shown: front, back and both sides. They are usually named after the direction they face, such as the north elevation. Elevations do not have to be drawn in any special layout – just arranged neatly on the page.

You can see below how to show doors and windows on elevations.

Window   **Door**

Puzzle

See if you can work out and draw the layout of the flat described on the right.

To find out if you were right, look at the actual layout on page 94.

Small & Pricey Ltd.
Estate Agents

The flat has a total area of 12m x 8.5m. All the rooms have windows looking out over the front or back gardens.

The front door enters the L-shaped hall, from which all the rooms lead. On the left is the living room (6m x 5.5m). A door from the living room leads into the kitchen (4m x 3m), which overlooks the back garden. Next to the kitchen is the bathroom (3.5m x 2m). The main bedroom (5.5m x 4.5m), is situated at the front of the house, while the second bedroom (4.5m x 3.5m), overlooks the garden.

Isometric drawing

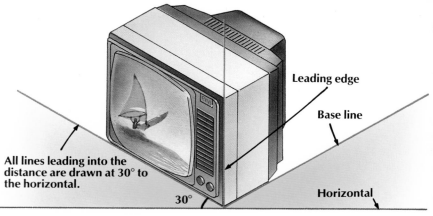

Leading edge

Base line

All lines leading into the distance are drawn at 30° to the horizontal.

30°

Horizontal

From an *orthographic projection*, it can be difficult to imagine what the object really looks like. To help visualize things, engineers and architects use a style of three-dimensional drawing, called *isometric projection*. Isometric projections are useful because they are quick and easy to draw.

The drawing above shows an isometric projection of a TV. Isometric drawings are not in *perspective*, so they look slightly distorted. Their advantage is that all the sides of an object are drawn at their true length, so you can take measurements from the finished drawing.

How to do an isometric drawing

These steps show how to do an isometric drawing. A video is shown, but you could draw any box-shaped object. Note down the object's measurements before you start.

Use a scale if the object is too big or small to be drawn full-size.

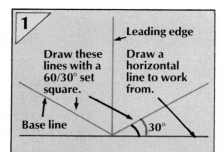

1

Leading edge

Draw these lines with a 60/30° set square.

Draw a horizontal line to work from.

Base line

30°

Draw a vertical line for the *leading edge* (the edge which appears to be closest to the viewer) and two *base lines*, at 30° to the horizontal.

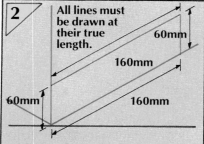

2

All lines must be drawn at their true length.

60mm

160mm

60mm

160mm

Mark the object's length and width along the base lines, and its height along the leading edge. Then construct the object's front face.

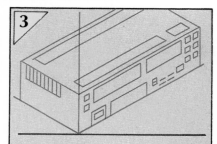

3

Draw the side and top in the same way. Horizontals are parallel to the base lines and verticals are parallel to the leading edge.

Irregular shapes

It is easier to draw objects with irregular shapes, like the chair shown on the right, if you first draw a box enclosing the object. This provides a framework to cut down on the number of *construction lines* needed, and helps position your drawing on the page. Draw the object's outline inside the box.

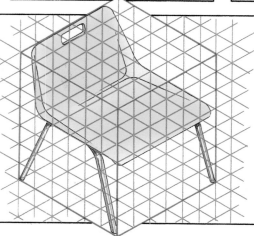

Isometric grid paper

Isometric *grid* paper is printed with vertical and 30° lines to make isometric drawing simple to do. The chair on the left is drawn on this kind of paper. You trace off the main outlines along the grid lines.

Exploded drawings

Exploded drawings show how the parts of an object fit together, by drawing them hovering in space around the object. Isometric exploded drawings are often used, as they are easier than drawing in perspective, and give true dimensions.

This simple exploded drawing shows the parts of a pencil sharpener. In isometric drawings circular parts like the hole and the screw are drawn in a special way. The steps below show you how.

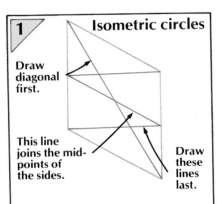

1   Isometric circles

Draw diagonal first.

This line joins the mid-points of the sides.

Draw these lines last.

Draw an isometric square with sides the same length as the circle's diameter. Then draw in the lines shown in blue.

2

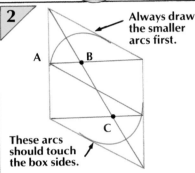

Always draw the smaller arcs first.

A   B

C

These arcs should touch the box sides.

Set your compasses to the length AB. With the point on B, draw an *arc*. With the same radius and the point on C, draw a second arc.

3

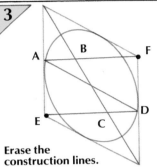

A   B   F

E   C   D

Erase the construction lines.

Set your compasses to the length ED. Put the point at E and draw an arc to touch the box sides. Draw a second arc with the point at F.

How you can use isometric drawings

An isometric drawing is an easy way to draw your own designs in three dimensions. Try drawing exciting buildings or your own inventions, like the spacecraft shown here. The steps below show how to construct a drawing like this*.

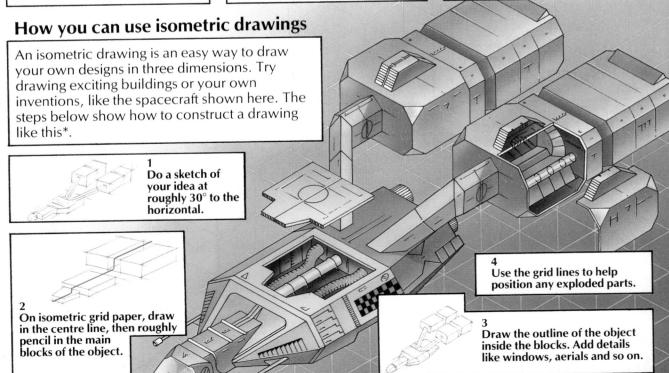

1
Do a sketch of your idea at roughly 30° to the horizontal.

2
On isometric grid paper, draw in the centre line, then roughly pencil in the main blocks of the object.

4
Use the grid lines to help position any exploded parts.

3
Draw the outline of the object inside the blocks. Add details like windows, aerials and so on.

*There are tips on how to colour drawings like this on pages 76-79.

Perspective drawing

Perspective is a method of drawing solid objects to make them look realistic. It attempts to reproduce what is seen in real life. Perspective is widely used for presentation drawings (drawings that a designer shows to a client), as it is the simplest way to show what something will actually look like.

Vanishing points

Horizon line

Vanishing point

Vanishing point

Extend these lines.

On the picture above, if you extend all the lines leading into the distance (called *receding lines*) you can see that they meet at two points. These are called *vanishing points*, and they are always situated on the *horizon*.

There are two main methods of perspective drawing: *one-point*, which has one vanishing point; and *two-point*, which has two vanishing points. You can find out more about the two methods on these pages.

Viewpoints and horizon

Horizon

The horizon is always in line with the viewer's eye level. If you are standing on flat ground, the horizon naturally falls about half-way up the scene.

Horizon

On a hill, you have a high viewpoint, so the horizon falls near the top of what you see. A high horizon makes your subject look small or far off.

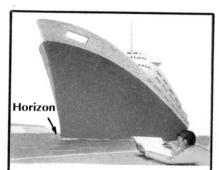

Horizon

On the ground, you have a low viewpoint, so the horizon falls near the bottom of what you see. A low horizon makes a subject look large or close up.

One-point perspective

One-point is the simplest perspective, and is used to show head-on views, such as interior views in architecture.

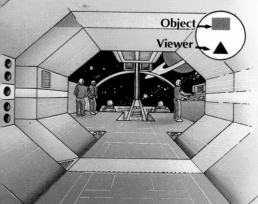

Object

Viewer

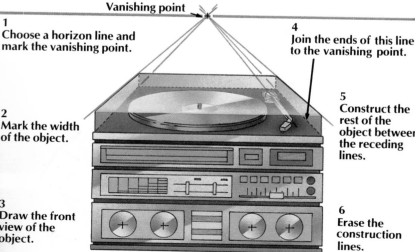

Vanishing point

1
Choose a horizon line and mark the vanishing point.

2
Mark the width of the object.

3
Draw the front view of the object.

4
Join the ends of this line to the vanishing point.

5
Construct the rest of the object between the receding lines.

6
Erase the construction lines.

Two-point perspective

Two-point perspective is used to draw objects which are at an angle to the viewer like the house on the right.

In two-point perspective there are two vanishing points: the left and the right-hand vanishing point. These are often abbreviated to VPL and VPR.

The steps below show how to construct a drawing in this type of perspective.

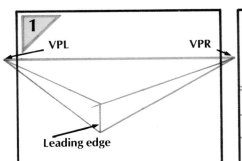

1

VPL   VPR

Leading edge

Draw the horizon line and two vanishing points, then mark in the *leading edge*. Join the ends of the leading edge to the two vanishing points.

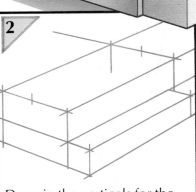

2

Draw in the verticals for the front and side views. Complete the outline by joining the ends to the opposite vanishing points.

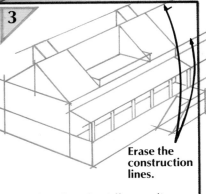

3

Erase the construction lines.

Add the details. All receding lines are constructed by joining the verticals to the vanishing points.

Viewpoint in two-point perspective

In a two-point drawing, the viewpoint is governed by the position of the leading edge in relation to the horizon line.

Placing the leading edge below the horizon gives the impression of looking down on the subject.

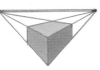

If the leading edge is *bisected* by the horizon line, you appear to be viewing the subject straight on.

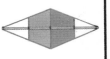

Placing the leading edge above the horizon gives the impression of looking up at the subject.

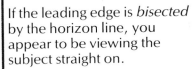

Positioning the vanishing points

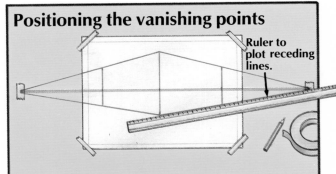

Ruler to plot receding lines.

To avoid distortion, it is best to position the vanishing points as far apart as possible. If the vanishing points are on the paper, you will end up with a small drawing in the middle and lots of blank space. You can avoid this by positioning the vanishing points on your drawing board or table and marking them with masking tape.

73

Using perspective

Circles in perspective

Minor axis

Major axis

A circle in *perspective* appears to be an oval shape, called an *ellipse*. An ellipse has two *axes*: the major axis along its length, and the minor axis along its width. There are several ways of drawing them, explained on this page.

Drawing ellipses freehand

It is often easiest to draw small ellipses freehand*. The motorcycle wheel on the right was first drawn in this way. Draw a box first as a framework, then sketch in the ellipse.

The ellipse touches the box at the mid-point of each side.

An ellipse always has rounded ends – not pointed ones.

---

1. Constructing an ellipse

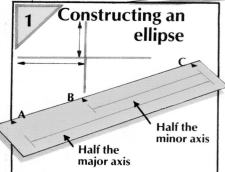

C

B

A

Half the minor axis

Half the major axis

Draw the major and minor axes, intersecting at 90°. Cut a strip of paper with a straight edge to use as a trammel**, and mark it as shown above.

2

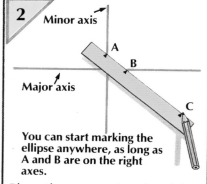

Minor axis

A
B

Major axis

C

You can start marking the ellipse anywhere, as long as A and B are on the right axes.

Place the trammel so that A is on the minor axis and B on the major axis, then mark the position of C with a pencil.

3

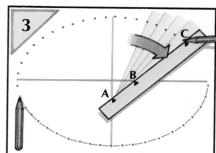

C

B

A

Gradually move the trammel around, keeping A and B on the axes. Plot the position of C as you go, as points to form an outline. Then join the points freehand.

---

1. Making an elliptical photo frame

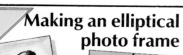

Allow at least 30mm border all round.

Leave a bigger border at the bottom.

Measure your photo to work out the size of elliptical hole needed. Cut a piece of stiff paper big enough for the ellipse and a border all round.

2

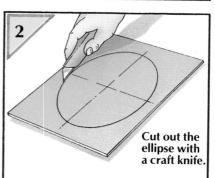

Cut out the ellipse with a craft knife.

Measure and pencil in the major and minor ellipse axes in the centre of the paper. Then draw the ellipse by the trammel method shown above.

3

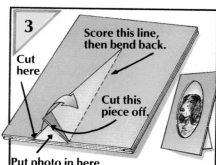

Score this line, then bend back.

Cut here

Cut this piece off.

Put photo in here.

Cut a piece of card the same size as the frame. Cut a support from the card as shown above. Stick the frame to the card with glue round the top and sides.

You could also use an ellipse guide – see page 87.
**The name trammel comes from a piece of drawing equipment used for drawing circles and ellipses.*

Using a perspective framework

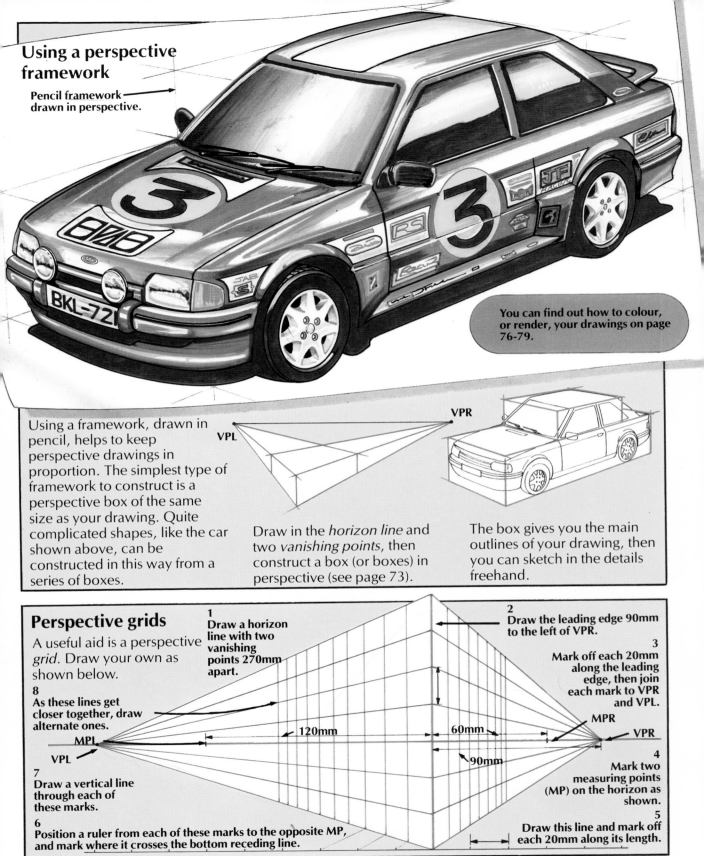

Pencil framework drawn in perspective.

You can find out how to colour, or render, your drawings on page 76-79.

Using a framework, drawn in pencil, helps to keep perspective drawings in proportion. The simplest type of framework to construct is a perspective box of the same size as your drawing. Quite complicated shapes, like the car shown above, can be constructed in this way from a series of boxes.

VPL

VPR

Draw in the *horizon line* and two *vanishing points*, then construct a box (or boxes) in perspective (see page 73).

The box gives you the main outlines of your drawing, then you can sketch in the details freehand.

Perspective grids

A useful aid is a perspective *grid*. Draw your own as shown below.

1 Draw a horizon line with two vanishing points 270mm apart.

2 Draw the leading edge 90mm to the left of VPR.

3 Mark off each 20mm along the leading edge, then join each mark to VPR and VPL.

4 Mark two measuring points (MP) on the horizon as shown.

5 Draw this line and mark off each 20mm along its length.

6 Position a ruler from each of these marks to the opposite MP, and mark where it crosses the bottom receding line.

7 Draw a vertical line through each of these marks.

8 As these lines get closer together, draw alternate ones.

120mm

60mm

90mm

MPL

VPL

MPR

VPR

75

Rendering techniques

Designers usually *render*, or colour, drawings that will be presented to clients, as this makes the drawings look much more exciting and realistic, and gives the impression of three dimensions.

There are lots of different rendering techniques, using pencils, pens and paints, which are explained on the next four pages. It is a good idea to practise on some rough paper before you start.

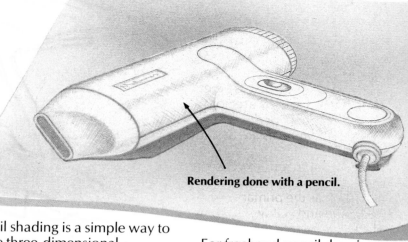

Rendering done with a pencil.

Pencil shading is a simple way to make three-dimensional drawings look convincingly realistic.

For freehand pencil drawing and shading use cartridge paper and a soft pencil (a B or softer).

---

1 Pencil shading

Hold the pencil between your thumb and first finger.

Hold the pencil as shown above. This puts the lead at a low angle to the paper, and lets you take longer and looser strokes, which are easier.

2 This side does not have shadows.   This side is shaded.

Shading is a way of showing areas in shadow. Decide where the light is coming from, then shade areas which face away from it.

3 Highlight   Hatching   Cross-hatching

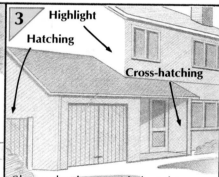

Show shadows with *hatching* (close parallel lines) or cross-hatching. Show bright areas, called highlights, by leaving the paper blank.

---

1 Coloured pencils

The techniques used for coloured pencils are the same as for lead pencils. Sketch out your drawing in lead pencil first, then fill it in with coloured pencils.

2

Mix colours by shading or cross-hatching one on top of another, as shown above. Keep a constant direction to your hatching lines rather than scribbling.

3

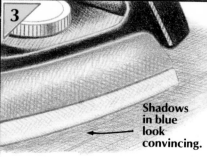

Shadows in blue look convincing.

Draw shaded areas by going over them in a slightly darker shade of the same colour. A white crayon is useful for highlights (parts which catch the light).

Marker pens

Markers are thick felt pens which are ideal for quick sketches, big illustrations and filling in large blocks of colour. Because they are so thick, markers are not suitable for small or detailed work. Fibre tip pens are best for finer work.

Markers are quite expensive, so it is best to buy just a few at first, such as the primary colours (red, blue and yellow), grey and black. Always recap your markers after use to prevent them drying out.

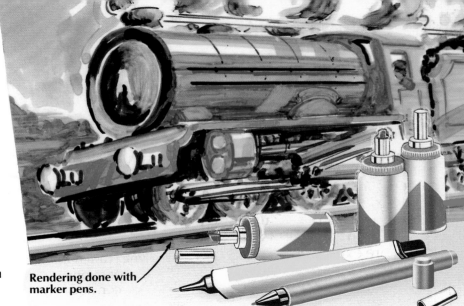

Rendering done with marker pens.

Choosing paper

Glue to stick tracing paper to white paper.

Mount tracing paper on white paper to show up the colours.

Markers bleed on ordinary paper. This spoils outlines and stains the lower sheets of a pad. Tracing paper or special bleedproof marker paper are best, as they do not let the colour soak through.

Using the tip

1

Use the narrowest edge for drawing and outlining.

2

Use the widest surface for colouring in large areas.

Markers have a chisel tip, which gives different line thicknesses according to how you hold the pen (see above). To get an even tone, it is best to colour quickly from side to side. Keep the marker tip moving all the time to stop it blotting.

Darker tones

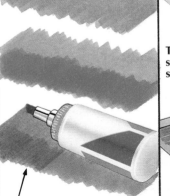

Make sure each layer is dry before you colour over it.

You can get different *tones* (shades of one colour) from a marker by colouring an area two or three times. This technique is useful for showing areas in shadow. Darker areas can also be made by going over the original colour in light grey.

Masking

Test the tape first to make sure it does not damage the surface of your paper.

Tidy up uneven edges with a coloured pencil.

Masking tape is useful if you want to make a straight edge. Stick tape along the edge, then colour from side to side across the tape, not along it. Peel the tape away when the ink is dry. Colour may bleed slightly under the tape.

More rendering techniques

Watercolours

Watercolour paints are used to *render* presentation drawings and as washes (watery layers of paint), to make parts of a drawing stand out. Washes are often used in architectural drawing.

Cartridge paper is best for watercolour rendering. Stretch it* first, otherwise it will cockle when it gets damp.

Washes

Start a wash at the top of the drawing and work downwards. Fill your brush and use long horizontal brush strokes to bring the wash down the drawing. Use a damp brush to remove any excess wash.

Stick masking tape round the paintbrush handle to give a better grip.

Use the brush to draw the wash along.

Draw the bristles to a point for a thin line.

Make darker tones by laying one wash of colour over another. Leave the colour to dry before painting on top.

The best watercolour brushes are made of sable and are expensive, but you can get good nylon brushes which are much cheaper.

Paint round the edges with a thin brush first, then fill in the rest of the shape with a larger brush.

Mix colours with a wet brush in the lid of your paint box or on a palette. Never mix colours on the picture.

Sticky-backed coloured paper

Peel off the excess paper.

Backing paper

You can buy special sticky-backed coloured paper and film in art shops. It is useful for filling in large areas of flat colour on models or drawings.

Draw the outline, then cut a piece of paper big enough to cover the shape. Peel off the backing and stick the paper down. Trim with a scalpel.

You can create different tones and colours by sticking one piece of paper on top of another. Draw details on top of the paper.

Colour and tone

There are three primary colours: red, yellow and blue. These can not be made from other colours, but they can be mixed together to create all other colours.

There are three secondary colours: orange, green and purple, which are made by mixing two primary colours.

Colour wheel   Primary colour

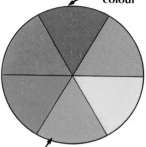

Secondary colour

Each secondary is a mixture of the primaries on either side.

Complementary colours

Colours opposite each other on the colour wheel are called complementary colours. Placing complementary colours together gives a very vivid effect.

Tone

The lightness or darkness of a colour is called its tone. Black and white photos show tone well as all colours are reduced to different tones of grey.

Airbrush

An airbrush is a device for spraying paint. A simple modeller's airbrush is useful for filling in large areas of colour and painting models. An artist's airbrush is expensive, but does very detailed work*.

You also need a compressed air supply, called a propellant. You can get aerosol cans of propellant or a mains electricity air compressor. Only buy one if you do a lot of airbrushing.

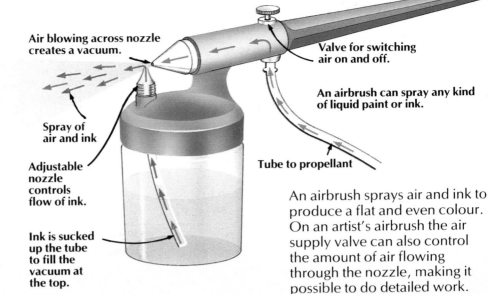

Air blowing across nozzle creates a vacuum.

Valve for switching air on and off.

Spray of air and ink

An airbrush can spray any kind of liquid paint or ink.

Adjustable nozzle controls flow of ink.

Tube to propellant

Ink is sucked up the tube to fill the vacuum at the top.

An airbrush sprays air and ink to produce a flat and even colour. On an artist's airbrush the air supply valve can also control the amount of air flowing through the nozzle, making it possible to do detailed work.

Using an airbrush

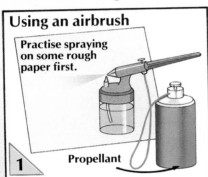

Practise spraying on some rough paper first.

Propellant

1 Fill the bottle with ink and connect the air tube to the propellant. Practise spraying and adjust the nozzle until the ink flows evenly.

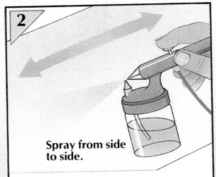

Spray from side to side.

2 For large areas, keep the airbrush moving all the time so the colour is even. Do not spray close to the paper or the ink will form a puddle.

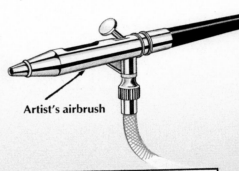

Artist's airbrush

Cleaning an airbrush

It is important to clean an airbrush each time you change inks as well as after using it. Any dried ink or grit in the tubes will prevent it spraying evenly.

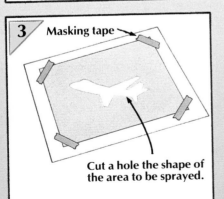

3 Masking tape

Cut a hole the shape of the area to be sprayed.

You need a mask to get a neat outline. Cut one from paper or card** to cover areas you do not want to colour.

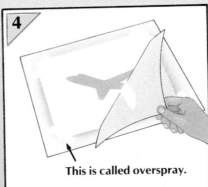

4 This is called overspray.

Spray from side to side across the paper over the edges of the mask. Wait until the paint is dry, then remove the mask.

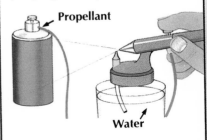

Propellant

Water

Empty the ink container and spray any remaining ink on to scrap paper. Fill the ink container with water, then spray this through the tubes to clean them out.

*Most of the illustrations in this book were done with an airbrush.
**You can get special masking film which peels off without damaging your drawing.

Using photographs

Photographs are useful as reminders of what an object looks like (called reference material), to trace from and as backgrounds for your own drawings. Any kind of camera is useful, but those with close-up focus are best. Pictures from magazines can be used instead of specially-taken photographs, so your own camera is not essential.

Taking your own reference photos

If you are taking your own reference pictures, a black and white film is often best as the pictures are often clearer and sharper than colour. Take lots of photos from different viewpoints, as this will help you to decide which is the most suitable view for the final drawing.

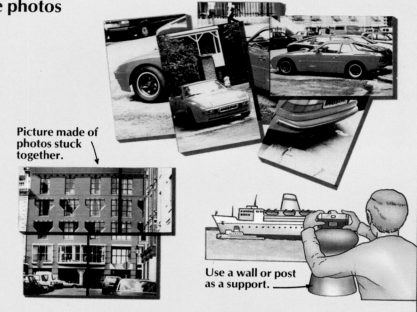

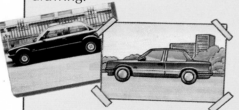

Picture made of photos stuck together.

Use a wall or post as a support.

Side and front views are useful, as these show true lengths and can be used to dimension your drawing. Dividers are useful for comparing proportions on the photo and the drawing.

The details in a photograph taken from a long way off will be blurred. To avoid this, take several overlapping photos, as close to the object as you can get, and stick them together as shown.

To take a series of overlapping photos, support the camera on something, so that the viewpoint will be the same in all the pictures. You could use a wall or post.

Photos as background

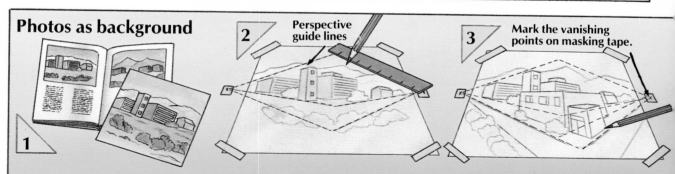

1

Take a background photo or use a picture from a magazine. You can enlarge these to a suitable size on a photocopier*.

2 Perspective guide lines

Place tracing paper over the photo. Draw in the *receding lines* of buildings or objects in the photo. Project the *vanishing points* from these lines.

3 Mark the vanishing points on masking tape.

Using the *perspective* guide lines, do your drawing on the tracing paper. Trace this on to drawing paper, cut it out and glue it to the photo.

Libraries and office stationery shops often have photocopying facilities.

Tracing from a photograph

Tracing from a photograph or a picture is an easy way to get an accurate outline of an object without setting up the perspective yourself. The steps below show you how.

You can either ink in the outline with a technical pen, or render it in colour. Inking in is a good way to practise using technical pens, which are often used to outline engineering and architectural drawings.

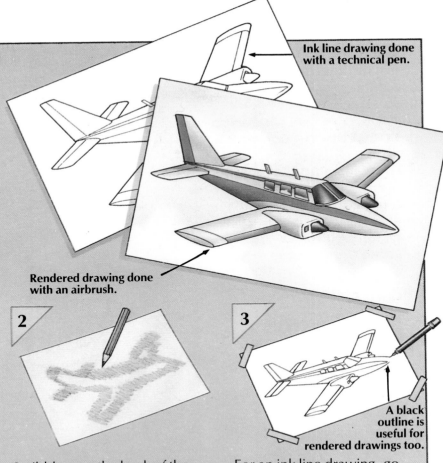

Ink line drawing done with a technical pen.

Rendered drawing done with an airbrush.

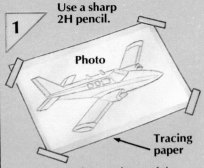

1 Use a sharp 2H pencil.

Photo

Tracing paper

Trace over the outline of the object. Miss out unnecessary details, shadows or reflections. Try to keep a steady hand so the lines will be straight.

2

Scribble over the back of the tracing with a soft pencil. Put the tracing over your drawing paper, and go over the outline again, this time with a 2H pencil.

3

A black outline is useful for rendered drawings too.

For an ink line drawing, go over the outline with a technical pen or thin felt pen. You could also use the tracing as an outline for a rendered drawing.

4

Render your drawing. If using a photocopied background render this too. Don't use marker pens, as they contain solvent which smudges photocopies.

Photographs vs drawings

*A photo is not usually focused all over, and some parts can be quite blurred. In a drawing the focus is sharp all over.

*In a photo you get a lot of objects in the background which you may not want. In a drawing you can choose your own background.

*Some camera lenses distort the shape of objects, especially near the edge of the picture.

No unwanted background.

Drawings can show how an object works.

*A photo can only show the object as it actually is, whereas a drawing can depict the object for a particular purpose, such as to show how it works.

Finishing touches

People react favourably to well-presented drawings. Using mounts and frames makes your drawings look professional and need not cost much, as you can make them yourself from paper or card.

There are some useful tips on these pages to help you present your drawings in a neat and professional way, both for exhibitions and for keeping them yourself.

Mounting drawings

A mount is a piece of card used to display a drawing. The simplest way to mount a drawing is to stick it to a thick paper or card backing, using one of the glues described on this page.

It is a good idea to cut out a damaged or dirtied drawing, and stick it to a fresh sheet of paper before mounting. Use a scalpel to trim carefully round the outline.

Glue

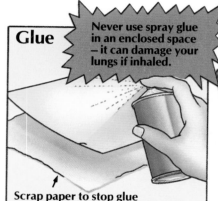

Never use spray glue in an enclosed space – it can damage your lungs if inhaled.

Scrap paper to stop glue getting on table.

Several types of glue are suitable for mounting. The easiest to use is spray glue. Glues which do not bond on contact are good as you can reposition anything crooked.

Cow gum

Cow gum sticks on contact, so you cannot adjust things.

Spread the glue thinly and evenly over both surfaces with a spatula or piece of card. Leave the glue for a few minutes to dry, then stick the surfaces together.

Double-sided tape

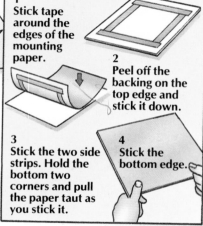

1 Stick tape around the edges of the mounting paper.

2 Peel off the backing on the top edge and stick it down.

3 Stick the two side strips. Hold the bottom two corners and pull the paper taut as you stick it.

4 Stick the bottom edge.

Window mounts

A window mount is a piece of paper or card with a "window" cut in it to make a frame. It is glued to the edges of a drawing.

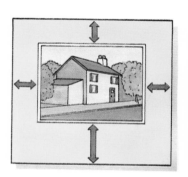

A window mount can be any shape, but it looks best if the frame is the same width at the sides and top, and wider at the bottom.

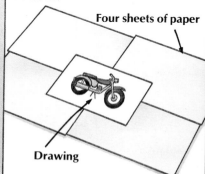

Four sheets of paper

Drawing

Adjust paper to the right size.

Work out the size of your mount with some rough paper as shown above. Then take measurements to transfer to the card.

Protecting drawings

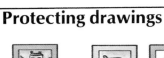

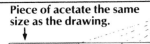

Piece of acetate the same size as the drawing.

Paper mask 10mm smaller than the acetate all round.

It is a good idea to protect display drawings from fingerprints and other marks with a layer of clear film. This also makes your drawings look professional.

Acetate is the easiest film to use as it can be stuck on with glue, but it is quite expensive. Apply glue round the edges of the acetate as shown above by masking with a piece of paper.

Drawings can also be laminated (sealed between two sheets of plastic) to protect them. You can get your drawings laminated at an instant print shop.

Stretching paper

Drawings *rendered* in watercolour work best on stretched cartridge paper. This prevents the paper cockling (wrinkling) as the paint dries.

1

Immerse the paper in a bowl of clean water. Shake the drips off, and place the paper flat on a wooden drawing board.

2

Stick the paper to the board with gummed brown paper tape round all the edges. Mop off excess water with a sponge.

3

Cut the paper off with a scalpel when your painting is finished and dry.

Keeping a portfolio

A portfolio is useful to protect your drawings. You can buy them from art or graphics shops, but they can be expensive. The steps below will show you how to make your own from card.

4
Cover the portfolio with coloured paper or sticky-backed plastic. The flaps must be folded in as you cover them otherwise they will not close.

1
Cut two A2 size pieces of stiff card.

2
Cut three flaps of card to fit the sides, as shown.

3
Tape the flaps to one piece of card, then tape the two pieces together.

5
Punch holes in the two side flaps and through the lid and base.

6
Tie a piece of tape through each of the holes, as fasteners.

How a professional designer works

Technical drawings and models are a vital stage in the design of new products, such as cars, washing machines and radios. They help to decide many things about the product, such as its final size and shape.

Here you can find out how a design team helps to develop a new car. The same principles apply to the design of any new product.

The research stage

Before the design team set to work the company does some market research. They ask customers questions to see what kind of car there is a demand for.

The company's engineers provide technical information on the materials to be used, the equipment available for building the car and aerodynamic shapes.

The design stages

1

The design team are given a brief (some instructions) made up of the market research ideas and the engineering specifications.

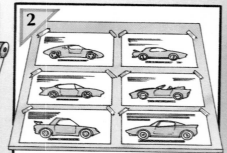

2

First the design team do a series of sketches to experiment with different ideas to show what the car might look like, both inside and outside.

3

Marker pens are often used for rendering cars.

Next they produce *rendered perspective* drawings of the most successful sketches. These are presented to the head designers, who decide which ideas are best.

4

Before a model is made, a designer does an *orthographic projection*. This gives more precise information about the car's size and shape.

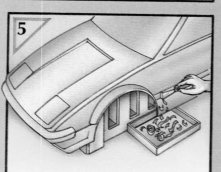

5

Next the ideas are presented to the company's managers, and one design is selected. The team then make a full-size clay model of the selected car design.

6

If the clay model is unsatisfactory, the design team make more sketches and models until everyone is happy with the design.

7

Computer-controlled measuring machine

A computer-controlled machine takes measurements from the final clay model. These are stored in the computer and are later used to make the car parts.

8

Next a full-size glass fibre model of the chosen design is made. The market research department shows this to customers to see if they like the car.

9

Light pen

Engineers call up diagrams of parts of the car on a computer terminal and make any minor adjustments with a light pen. This is called *CAD – computer-aided design*

10

"Wire-frame" diagram

When all the parts are designed, the complete body structure can be seen on the computer terminal as a "wire-frame" diagram.

11

Designers use the "wire-frame" diagram to test for stress points and how the car would react in a crash. The design is then modified if necessary.

12

A prototype car is built from the information in the computer. It is tested for safety, durability, noise levels, rusting and extreme weather conditions.

Making the car

When the prototype has been adjusted to pass all the tests, production of the actual car can start.

Technical drawing equipment

On these pages there is a list of all the basic materials and equipment mentioned in this book, together with suggestions about more advanced equipment to buy if you have a little more money to spend.

You can also read about the different paper sizes that are available and the range of pencil hardnesses to choose from.

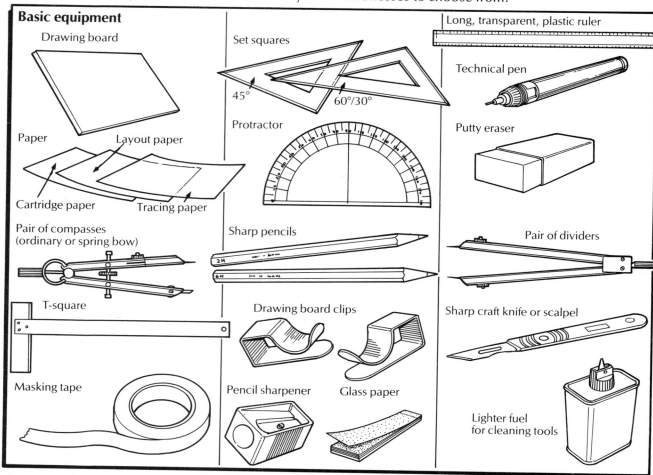

Basic equipment

Drawing board

Set squares

45° 60°/30°

Long, transparent, plastic ruler

Technical pen

Paper

Layout paper

Cartridge paper Tracing paper

Protractor

Putty eraser

Pair of compasses (ordinary or spring bow)

Sharp pencils

Pair of dividers

T-square

Drawing board clips

Sharp craft knife or scalpel

Masking tape

Pencil sharpener Glass paper

Lighter fuel for cleaning tools

Paper sizes

Sheets of paper come in two ranges of sizes: traditional sizes*(such as foolscap, crown and demy) and the internationally used "A" series. A size paper is normally used for technical drawing.

The system is based on the AO size, which has an area of one square metre. The other sizes in the series (A1, A2, A3 etc) are all obtained from the basic AO size, each one being half the area of the previous size (see the diagram on the right).

A3 is the best size for most technical drawings.

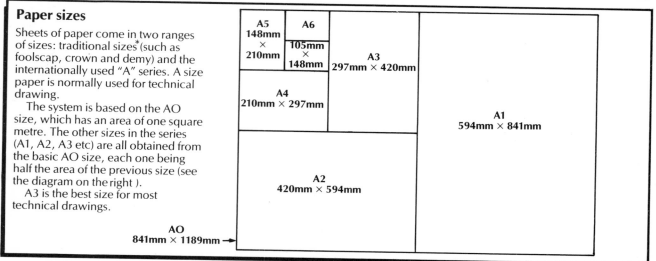

A5 148mm × 210mm

A6 105mm × 148mm

A3 297mm × 420mm

A4 210mm × 297mm

A2 420mm × 594mm

A1 594mm × 841mm

AO 841mm × 1189mm →

*These sizes are no longer widely used.

Advanced equipment

 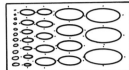

Ellipse and circle guides: templates for drawing *ellipses* and circles.

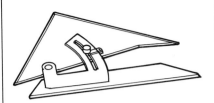

Adjustable set square: this can be adjusted to measure any angle between 45° and 90°.

French curves: used to draw curved lines.

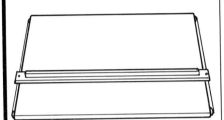

Parallel motion drawing board; this has a fitted T-square which moves up and down on a pulley system.

Scale rules: these are used when drawing to *scale*. They are divided up according to the most commonly used scales.

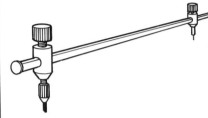

Beam compass: a special compass for drawing large circles. The pencil fitting is screwed to a horizontal bar to give a large radius.

Ruling pen: an adjustable ink pen used to draw lines of different thickness. These are difficult to use – technical pens are easier.

Flexible curves: lengths of pliable plastic which can be bent to any curve.

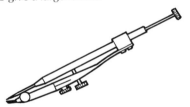

Drop compass: a compass for drawing very small circles.

Pencil hardnesses

Pencils are graded according to their hardness, from 9H to 7B. H stands for hard, and B stands for black. The pencil "lead" is actually made from a mixture of graphite (which makes the marks) and clay (which binds the graphite together). The more clay there is in the lead, the harder the pencil is.

The table below shows the range of pencils and what they are used for.

9H-5H: Extra hard – special pencils used for draughting.

4H and 3H: Very hard – used for *construction*, *dimension* and *projection lines*.

2H and H: Hard – used for *outlines* on technical drawings.

HB, B and 2B: Soft – used for freehand drawing and sketching.

3B-7B: Very soft – for shading.

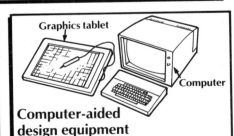

Computer-aided design equipment

Computers can help designers to work much faster than drawing with conventional equipment. This is called *computer-aided design* (CAD).

The designer uses a graphics tablet (an electronic drawing board linked to the computer), or a light pen, which can "draw" straight on to the screen. The computer stores the dimensions and can print out the drawing.

Geometry tips

Geometry is often used in technical drawing, to do things like dividing angles and lines in half. Below are some simple geometrical methods which you will often need to use in your drawings.

Bisecting an angle

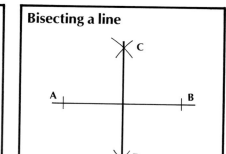

Bisect means divide in half.

This radius can be any length.

Put a compass point on A and mark off the *arcs* at B and C. Then put the compass point on B and C in turn and draw the two intersecting arcs at D. The line from A to D *bisects* the angle.

Bisecting a line

Set your compasses to more than half the length of the line to be bisected. Put the compass point at A and B in turn and mark the arcs at C and D. The line from C to D bisects AB.

Rounded corners

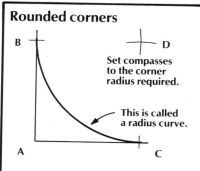

Set compasses to the corner radius required.

This is called a radius curve.

With the compass point at A, draw the arcs at B and C. Put the compass point at B and C in turn and draw the intersecting arcs at D. Then at D to draw an arc to touch the corner lines at B and C.

Drawing a hexagon

The radius will fit six times around the circumference.

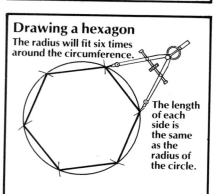

The length of each side is the same as the radius of the circle.

Draw a circle and with the same radius mark off arcs around the circumference as shown above. With a ruler join the six arcs to form a hexagon.

Drawing a perpendicular

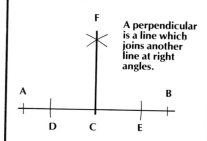

A perpendicular is a line which joins another line at right angles.

Set your compasses to a radius less than A to C. Put the point on C and mark the arcs at D and E. Then with a larger radius and the point on D and E in turn, mark the arcs at F. The line F to C is *perpendicular* to AB.

Things to draw

These optical illusions are easy to draw and good practice to get used to using your equipment. The steps below will show you how to draw them.

The horizontal lines are all ► parallel, although they do not look it. Draw them first, using a T-square. The sloping lines are at 30° to the horizontal – use a 60°/30° set square.

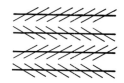

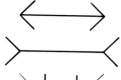

◄ The two horizontal lines are the same length, although one looks longer. Draw them first with a T-square and set square. Draw the arrows with a 45° set square.

The two black circles are the ► same size, although one appears larger than the other. Draw the black circles first, with the same radius, then add the surrounding circles.

◄ The two vertical lines are parallel, although they look curved. Mark off 15° divisions with a protractor, then draw in the radiating lines. Draw the two vertical lines either side of the centre.

Studio tips

Using tracing paper

If a drawing does not look right first time, do not throw it away. Trace the *layout* or the good parts on to fresh paper to save having to start the whole drawing from scratch.

Bevelled instruments

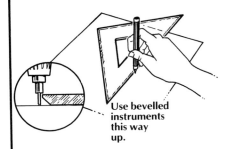

Use bevelled instruments this way up.

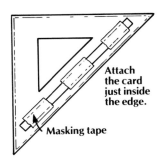

Attach the card just inside the edge.

Masking tape

A *bevel* is a sloping edge on drawing instruments which makes it easier to ink lines. It prevents smudging as it keeps the instruments away from the ink line. There are bevels on rulers, set squares and protractors.

If your equipment does not have bevelled edges, you can get the same effect by sticking on a strip of card, as shown above. Attach the card securely with masking tape or double-sided tape.

Inking in lines

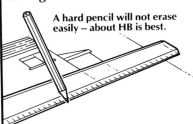

A hard pencil will not erase easily – about HB is best.

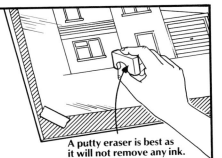

A putty eraser is best as it will not remove any ink.

It is best to mark out guidelines in pencil first to show where the ink lines will go. Keep your lines very faint, and draw as little as possible – points or dashes are often enough to indicate the position of a line.

Ink over the lines with a technical pen. If the ink does not flow evenly, shake the pen from side to side horizontally. Leave the ink to dry thoroughly before you erase any pencil *construction lines* that show through.

Drying drawings

Hairdryer

A hairdryer is useful for drying ink and paint drawings quickly. Keep the hairdryer nozzle well away from your drawing, otherwise you may cockle the paper or blow the wet ink around.

Keeping drawings clean

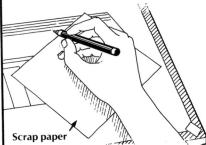

Scrap paper

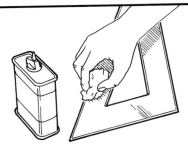

Cover paper

Stick paper to the back of the drawing.

Drawings look best if kept clean and smudge-free. Always wash your hands before starting and if you get any paint on them. Some scrap paper under your hand will stop you marking the drawing paper.

Tissue paper soaked in lighter fuel is useful for cleaning ink and other marks from your equipment. It will also remove greasy marks from drawings, but test your paper first to make sure it does not stain.

Always protect your unfinished drawings from dust and other marks. Either keep them in a portfolio*, or cover them with a sheet of paper, as shown above.

*You can find out how to make your own portfolio on page 83.

Drawing conventions

A *convention* is a standard way of representing features on technical drawings. On these pages you can find out about some of the conventions and about different ways of showing *dimensions* and sections on drawings. There is also a list of common abbreviations, and information about when to use different kinds of lines on your drawings.

Abbreviations

Abbrev-iation	Meaning	Symbol						
A/F	Across flats		DIA ∅	Diameter: in a note before a dimension	ISO	International standards organization	RAD R	Radius: in a note before a dimension
A/F	Across flats		DRG	Drawing	LH	Left hand	:	Ratio
C, CL or c	Centre line		EXT	External	MAX	Maximum	RH	Right hand
CH HD	Cheese head		HEX HD	Hexagonal head	MPL MPR	Measuring point left/right	SK	Sketch
CAD	Computer-aided design		I/D	Inside diameter	MIN	Minimum	SWG	Standard wire gauge
					NTS	Not to scale		
CSK HD	Countersunk head		INT	Internal	O/D	Outside diameter	VP VPL VPR	Vanishing point Left-hand Right-hand

Dimensions have to be clearly shown on technical drawings. The usual way of doing this is to draw dimension lines (see page 65) and to write the dimension above the middle of the line. Below you can find out about special methods used to dimension circles, radius curves and angles.

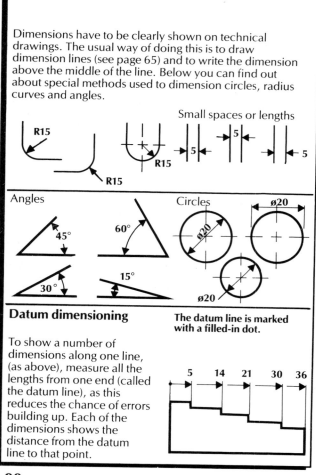

Datum dimensioning

To show a number of dimensions along one line, (as above), measure all the lengths from one end (called the datum line), as this reduces the chance of errors building up. Each of the dimensions shows the distance from the datum line to that point.

The datum line is marked with a filled-in dot.

Lines used in technical drawing

The table below shows the main lines used in technical drawing, and where you use them.

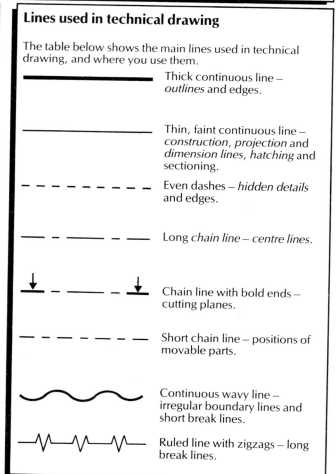

Architectural conventions

Below you can find out the conventional methods of representing features on architectural drawings.

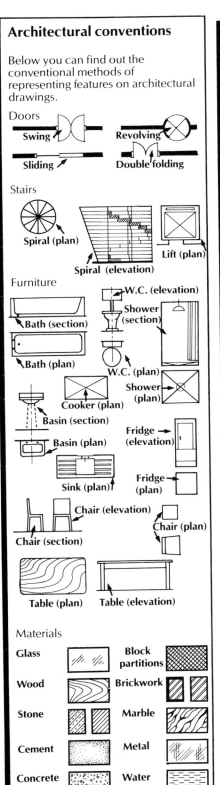

Doors

Swing

Revolving

Sliding

Double folding

Stairs

Spiral (plan)

Lift (plan)

Spiral (elevation)

Furniture

Bath (section)

W.C. (elevation)

Shower (section)

Bath (plan)

W.C. (plan)

Cooker (plan)

Shower (plan)

Basin (section)

Fridge (elevation)

Basin (plan)

Sink (plan)

Fridge (plan)

Chair (elevation)

Chair (plan)

Chair (section)

Table (plan)

Table (elevation)

Materials

Glass		Block partitions	
Wood		Brickwork	
Stone		Marble	
Cement		Metal	
Concrete		Water	

Engineering conventions

The drawings below show the conventional ways of representing standard features on engineering drawings.

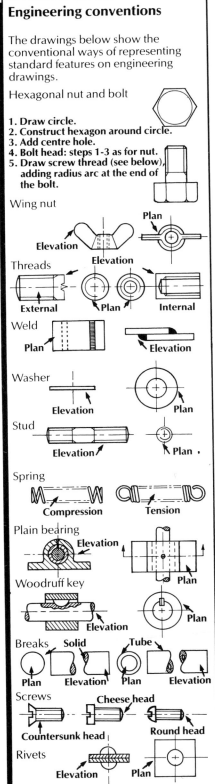

Hexagonal nut and bolt

1. Draw circle.
2. Construct hexagon around circle.
3. Add centre hole.
4. Bolt head: steps 1-3 as for nut.
5. Draw screw thread (see below), adding radius arc at the end of the bolt.

Wing nut

Plan

Elevation

Threads

Elevation

External

Plan

Internal

Weld

Plan

Elevation

Washer

Elevation

Plan

Stud

Elevation

Plan

Spring

Compression

Tension

Plain bearing

Elevation

Plan

Woodruff key

Elevation

Plan

Breaks

Solid

Tube

Plan

Elevation

Plan

Elevation

Screws

Cheese head

Countersunk head

Round head

Rivets

Elevation

Plan

Sections

A section is a view of an object cut open along a marked line to show internal details. There are different types of section, which are described below. You may need several sections to show an object fully, just as you need more than one elevation.

If you cut an object horizontally, you get a horizontal or plan section.

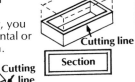

Cutting line

Section

Cutting line

Section

If you cut an object vertically along its length, you get a longitudinal section.

Cutting line

If you cut an object vertically across its width, you get a cross section.

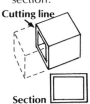

Section

Revolved sections

These are sections which are rotated (usually by 90°) so that you can see more of the object on the section.

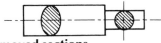

Removed sections

Sections are normally projected from their original elevation. Removed sections are those which are positioned elsewhere on the drawing. They can be drawn to a larger scale, which makes dimensioning easier.

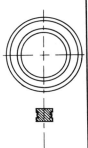

Half sections

These are drawings which show half the object as an outside view and half of it as a section.

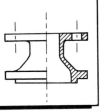

91

Model plans

These plans are for the models on pages 58 and 59. Either copy the plans at the same size by photocopying or tracing them, or enlarge them by following the instructions on page 94.

Draw and cut out each piece once. The solid black lines around the outside of each piece show where to cut. The dotted lines show where to make folds.

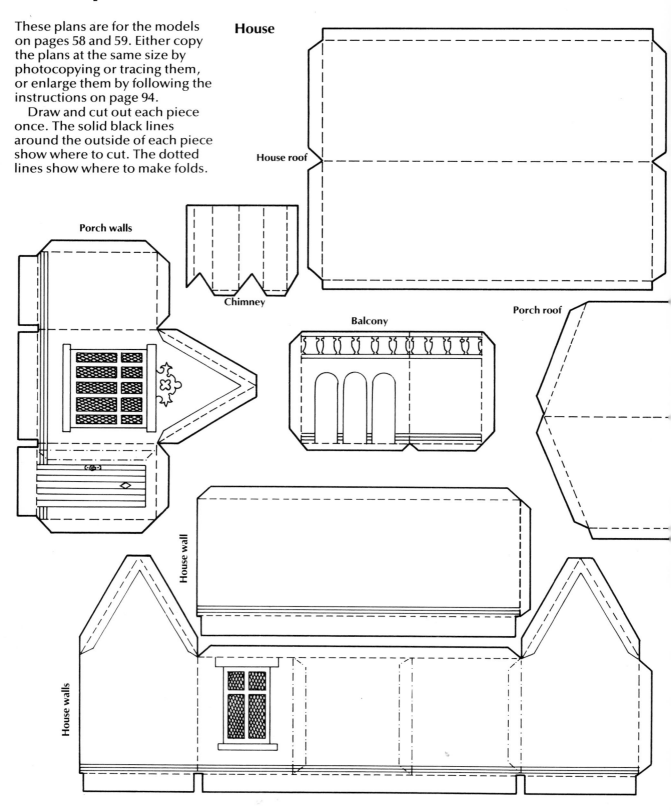

House

House roof

Porch walls

Chimney

Balcony

Porch roof

House wall

House walls

Truck

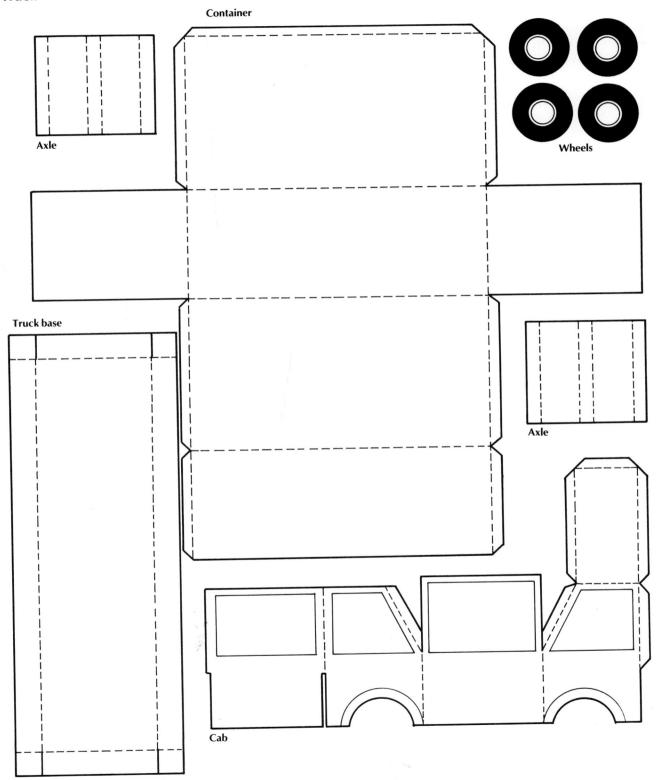

Axle

Container

Wheels

Truck base

Axle

Cab

Enlarging plans and other useful information

The tips below show how to enlarge or reduce drawings and plans using a grid. You can use this method to enlarge the plans for the model house and truck on page 92/93.

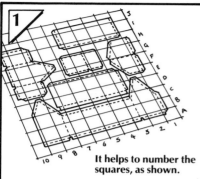

1

It helps to number the squares, as shown.

With a T-square and a set square, draw a light pencil grid over the plans, using 10mm or 20mm squares. Decide how much you want to enlarge the plans – to two or three times their original size, for example.

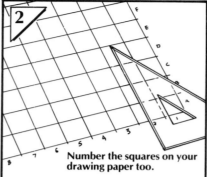

2

Number the squares on your drawing paper too.

Using a T-square and set square, divide your drawing paper into the same number of squares. If the drawing is to be twice as big, draw squares twice the size of those on the plans, and so on.

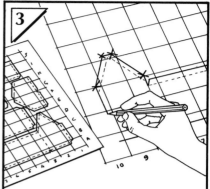

3

Copy what is in each square on the plan into the corresponding square on the paper. It is easiest to plot the points where the outlines cross the grid lines, and then join these points.

Going further

If you want to find out more about technical drawing and illustration, the books below may be useful.

For engineering drawing:

Engineering Drawing and Construction
by L.C. Mott
Oxford University Press, 1965.

Geometrical and Technical Drawing
by A. Yarwood
Nelson, 1983.

For architectural drawing:

Draughtsmanship
by Fraser Reekie
Edward Arnold, 1976.

Manual of Graphic Techniques
by Tom Porter and Sue Goodman
Astragal Books, 1985.

For perspective drawing:

Basic Perspective
by Robert W. Gill
Thames and Hudson, 1974.

For technical illustration:

Studio Tips and **More Studio Tips**
by Bill Gray
Van Nostrand Reinhold, 1976 and 1979.

Presentation Techniques
by Dick Powell
Orbis, 1985.

Answers to puzzles

Page 67

1. Plan view of a cassette tape.
2. Plan view of an aerosol can.
3. Side view of an alarm clock.
4. Plan view of a door handle
5. Plan view of a tap.
6. Side view of a ball point pen

Page 69

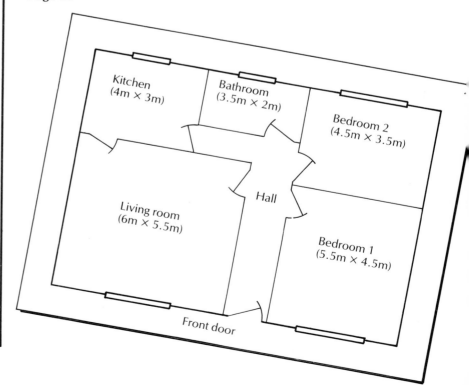

Kitchen (4m × 3m)

Bathroom (3.5m × 2m)

Bedroom 2 (4.5m × 3.5m)

Living room (6m × 5.5m)

Hall

Bedroom 1 (5.5m × 4.5m)

Front door

Glossary

Arc. Part of a circle's circumference.

Axis. An imaginary line through the centre of an object. For example, a line showing the length (major axis) or width (minor axis) of an *ellipse*.

Base line. A line at 30° to the horizontal, used for constructing *isometric* drawings.

Bevel. A sloping edge used on drawing instruments.

Bisect. To divide in half.

Centre lines. Thin *chain lines* used to mark the centre of circles, *arcs* and circular or *elliptical* parts.

Chain line. A line made up of alternate long and short dashes.

Computer-aided design (CAD). A computer system used in design.

Construction lines. Faint lines used to plot out basic shapes before drawing an *outline*.

Convention. A standard, internationally accepted method of representing something.

Design process. The stages a designer goes through to get from an initial idea to a finished product.

Development. A drawing showing all the surfaces of an object opened out on to one *plane*.

Dimensions. Measurements such as length and width. Dimension lines are used on drawings to show these measurements.

Elevation. In architecture, a two-dimensional drawing of the front or side of a building. In engineering, *front* and *side* views can also be called elevations.

Ellipse. An oval shape, or a circle viewed in *perspective*.

Exploded drawing. One which shows how the parts of an object fit together by showing them in space around the main piece.

First angle. Type of *orthographic projection* in which the left-hand *side view* is shown projected to the right of the *front view*, under which is the *plan view*.

Front view. Two-dimensional drawing of the front of an object, used in *orthographic projection*.

Grid. A framework of guide lines.

Hatching. Close parallel lines used for shading drawings.

Hidden details. Parts of an object which cannot be directly seen in a technical drawing. Their position is indicated by dashed lines.

Horizon line. The line where the sky appears to meet the earth. It is always at the viewer's eye level.

Isometric projection. A type of three-dimensional technical drawing in which *receding lines* are drawn at 30° to the horizontal.

Landscape. A rectangular piece of paper with the longer sides placed horizontally.

Layout. The arrangement of a drawing on the paper.

Leading edge. The vertical line which appears to be nearest the viewer in an *isometric or perspective* drawing.

Mock-up. A model.

One-point. Type of *perspective* drawing in which there is only one *vanishing point*.

Orthographic projection. Method of depicting an object by drawing a series of flat views of its different sides, arranged in a special layout.

Outline. A line showing the edges of the shape being drawn. Outlines are drawn with a continuous pencil line.

Perpendicular. A line which joins another line at 90°.

Perspective. Way of drawing solid objects to give an impression of depth and distance.

Plan view. Two-dimensional drawing of the top of an object, used in *orthographic projection*.

Plane. A flat surface.

Portrait. A rectangular piece of paper with the shorter sides placed horizontally.

Presentation drawing. One which a designer does to show a client what the design will look like.

Projection lines. Lines used in technical drawing to position *dimension lines* outside the main *outline*.

Quadrant. A quarter of a sphere or of a circle.

Ratio. A mathematical way of showing the proportion of one quantity to another, e.g. 2:1, means the drawing is twice as big as the original.

Receding lines. Lines in *perspective* and *isometric* drawings which appear to lead into the distance.

Rendering. Colouring or shading a drawing.

Scale. A method of drawing objects bigger or smaller than they are in real life, and of showing how much they have been enlarged or reduced. The scale is often shown as a *ratio*.

Side view. Two-dimensional drawing of the side of an object, used in *orthographic projection*.

Third angle. Type of *orthographic projection* in which the left-hand *side view* is shown to the left of the *front view*, above which is the *plan*.

Thumbnail sketch. A tiny sketch.

Tone. The degree of lightness or darkness of a colour.

Two-point. Method of *perspective* drawing in which there are two *vanishing points*.

Vanishing point. In *perspective* drawing, a point on the horizon at which the *receding lines* appear to meet.

Index